OPPOSING
VIEWPOINTS®
SERIES

Illegal Immigration

Other Books of Related Interest:

Opposing Viewpoints Series
Human Rights
Humanity's Future
Immigration
Interracial America

Current Controversies Series
Civil Rights
Developing Nations
Immigration

At Issue Series
Does Outsourcing Harm America?
Is the Political Divide Harming America?
Protecting the Nation's Borders
What Rights Should Illegal Immigrants Have?

"Congress shall make
no law ... abridging
the freedom of speech,
or of the press."

First Amendment to the U.S. Constitution

The basic foundation of our democracy is the First Amendment guarantee of freedom of expression. The Opposing Viewpoints Series is dedicated to the concept of this basic freedom and the idea that it is more important to practice it than to enshrine it.

Illegal Immigration

Margaret Haerens, Book Editor

GREENHAVEN PRESS

An imprint of Thomson Gale, a part of The Thomson Corporation

Detroit • New York • San Francisco • San Diego • New Haven, Conn.
Waterville, Maine • London • Munich

THOMSON
— ✳ — ™
GALE

Bonnie Szumski, *Publisher*
Helen Cothran, *Managing Editor*

© 2006 Thomson Gale, a part of The Thomson Corporation.

Thomson and Star Logo are trademarks and Gale and Greenhaven Press are registered trademarks used herein under license.

For more information, contact:
Greenhaven Press
27500 Drake Rd.
Farmington Hills, MI 48331-3535
Or you can visit our Internet site at http://www.gale.com

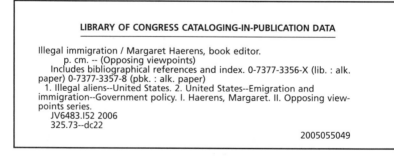

LIBRARY OF CONGRESS CATALOGING-IN-PUBLICATION DATA

Illegal immigration / Margaret Haerens, book editor.
   p. cm. -- (Opposing viewpoints)
   Includes bibliographical references and index. 0-7377-3356-X (lib. : alk. paper) 0-7377-3357-8 (pbk. : alk. paper)
   1. Illegal aliens--United States. 2. United States--Emigration and immigration--Government policy. I. Haerens, Margaret. II. Opposing viewpoints series.
   JV6483.I52 2006
   325.73--dc22

                                                        2005055049

Printed in the United States of America
10 9 8 7 6 5 4 3 2 1

Contents

Chapter 3: How Should America Enforce Its Borders?

Chapter 4: How Should U.S. Immigration Policy Be Reformed?

> *"The only way in which a human being can make some approach to knowing the whole of a subject is by hearing what can be said about it by persons of every variety of opinion and studying all modes in which it can be looked at by every character of mind. No wise man ever acquired his wisdom in any mode but this."*
>
> John Stuart Mill

Why Consider Opposing Viewpoints?

In our media-intensive culture it is not difficult to find differing opinions. Thousands of newspapers and magazines and dozens of radio and television talk shows resound with differing points of view. The difficulty lies in deciding which opinion to agree with and which "experts" seem the most credible. The more inundated we become with differing opinions and claims, the more essential it is to hone critical reading and thinking skills to evaluate these ideas. Opposing Viewpoints books address this problem directly by presenting stimulating debates that can be used to enhance and teach these skills. The varied opinions contained in each book examine many different aspects of a single issue. While examining these conveniently edited opposing views, readers can develop critical thinking skills such as the ability to compare and contrast authors' credibility, facts, argumentation styles, use of persuasive techniques, and other stylistic tools. In short, the Opposing Viewpoints Series is an ideal way to attain the higher-level thinking and reading skills so essential in a culture of diverse and contradictory opinions.

In addition to providing a tool for critical thinking, Opposing Viewpoints books challenge readers to question their own strongly held opinions and assumptions. Most people form their opinions on the basis of upbringing, peer pressure, and personal, cultural, or professional bias. By reading carefully balanced opposing views, readers must directly confront new ideas as well as the opinions of those with whom they disagree. This is not to simplistically argue that everyone who reads opposing views will—or should—change his or her opinion. Instead, the series enhances readers' understanding of their own views by encouraging confrontation with opposing ideas. Careful examination of others' views can lead to the readers' understanding of the logical inconsistencies in their own opinions, perspective on why they hold an opinion, and the consideration of the possibility that their opinion requires further evaluation.

Evaluating Other Opinions

To ensure that this type of examination occurs, Opposing Viewpoints books present all types of opinions. Prominent spokespeople on different sides of each issue as well as well-known professionals from many disciplines challenge the reader. An additional goal of the series is to provide a forum for other, less known, or even unpopular viewpoints. The opinion of an ordinary person who has had to make the decision to cut off life support from a terminally ill relative, for example, may be just as valuable and provide just as much insight as a medical ethicist's professional opinion. The editors have two additional purposes in including these less known views. One, the editors encourage readers to respect others' opinions—even when not enhanced by professional credibility. It is only by reading or listening to and objectively evaluating others' ideas that one can determine whether they are worthy of consideration. Two, the inclusion of such viewpoints encourages the important critical thinking skill of objectively evaluating an author's credentials and bias. This evaluation will illuminate an author's reasons for taking a particular stance on an issue and will aid in readers' evaluation of the author's ideas.

It is our hope that these books will give readers a deeper understanding of the issues debated and an appreciation of the complexity of even seemingly simple issues when good and honest people disagree. This awareness is particularly important in a democratic society such as ours in which people enter into public debate to determine the common good. Those with whom one disagrees should not be regarded as enemies but rather as people whose views deserve careful examination and may shed light on one's own.

Thomas Jefferson once said that "difference of opinion leads to inquiry, and inquiry to truth." Jefferson, a broadly educated man, argued that "if a nation expects to be ignorant and free ... it expects what never was and never will be." As individuals and as a nation, it is imperative that we consider the opinions of others and examine them with skill and discernment. The Opposing Viewpoints Series is intended to help readers achieve this goal.

David L. Bender and Bruno Leone,
Founders

Introduction

> *"To defend this country, we have to en-
> force our borders."*
> —*President George W. Bush*

The terrorist attacks of September 11, 2001, had a profound effect on America's approach to the already controversial issue of immigration. In the immediate aftermath of
the attacks, people demanded to know how the nineteen hijackers—all foreign nationals—who flew the planes that
crashed into the World Trade Center, the Pentagon, and a field
in Pennsylvania had gotten into the United States. An investigation of the hijackers showed that they had violated U.S. immigration laws in several ways. A few of the hijackers were
known al Qaeda operatives who should have been on a terrorist watch list. The terrorists' passports had been manipulated
and contained suspicious indicators. The hijackers had also
made detectable false statements on their visa applications and
to border officials in order to gain entry to the United States.
According to a report authored by Janice L. Kephart for the
Center for Immigration Studies, an immigration research organization, the September 11 attack "highlights the danger of
our lax immigration system, not just in terms of who is allowed in, but also how terrorists, once in the country, used
weaknesses in the system to remain here."

After the September 11 attacks, immigration became integral to the national debate over terrorism and national security. People from across the political spectrum argued that the
U.S. government needed to improve its ability to track people
entering on visas and make it more difficult for illegal immigrants to cross the border and remain in the country. A November 2003 poll by the Pew Research Center reported that

77 percent of Americans believed that "we should restrict and control people coming into the country to live more than we do now." A March 2003 poll by the Roper ASW organization reported that 85 percent of Americans thought that illegal immigration was a serious problem.

In an effort to protect America from foreign terrorism, the Bush administration made several immigration reforms. The Department of Homeland Security was put in charge of issuing and overseeing visas. In order to better track foreign visitors, the new US-VISIT system requires incoming visa holders to be fingerprinted and digitally photographed. In addition, illegal aliens have been added to the Federal Bureau of Investigation's National Crime Information Center (NCIC) database, which is widely used by state and local police.

Investigations into possible terrorist suspects led to arrests and deportations, sometimes on minor breaches of immigration policy. During the investigation of the hijackings, 768 suspects were secretly processed on immigration charges. Most of these individuals were deported after being cleared of connections to terrorist activity. Overall, more than 4.8 million illegal immigrants have been deported from the United States since 2001, including more than 300,000 with criminal records. Supporters of these efforts argue the United States must take whatever measures necessary to defend itself against terrorism. Therefore, immigration policy should be a key tool in the war on terror. Detaining and deporting illegal aliens, they contend, is only the first step in what should be a significant reform of U.S. immigration policy.

Critics charge that the crackdown on immigrants violates the civil rights of both legal and illegal immigrants. Many immigrants have been detained without legal representation in secret locations without due process of law because of minor violations of immigration law. Detractors also allege that these procedures are discriminatory because they focus more heavily on Muslims and Arabs than other nationalities. In the long term, they argue, these new laws and procedures will hurt the political, cultural, and economic interests of America.

The events of September 11, 2001, spotlighted the tension between the need to ensure the civil rights of immigrants and the importance of protecting America's national security. *Opposing Viewpoints: Illegal Immigration* explores this question as well as other issues in the following chapters: Does Illegal Immigration Harm America? Does the United States Treat Illegal Immigrants Fairly? How Should America Enforce Its Borders? How Should U.S. Immigration Policy Be Reformed? The viewpoints included in this book address these vital questions and provide a sampling of the sharp divisions that exist within this country regarding this controversial issue.

Does Illegal Immigration Harm America?

Chapter Preface

The United States is a country of immigrants. From the arrival of the Pilgrims in the seventeenth century to refugees fleeing religious and political persecution in the twenty-first century, immigration has played an essential role in the nation's success. As the country grew, America's exploding agricultural and industrial sectors needed the cheap labor provided by these constantly arriving immigrants. The new arrivals, both skilled and unskilled workers, helped to build America into a world power.

Illegal immigrants have always been welcomed by American businesses. These immigrants have usually been men who cross the border to work for a short period of time for a substandard wage. Employers save money by employing these unauthorized workers because they sometimes pay them off the books and therefore do not pay federal or state employment taxes. Moreover, illegal immigrants do not receive expensive job benefits, such as health insurance or disability insurance. In industries that require scores of cheap workers, such as construction and agriculture, illegal immigrants fulfill that need. It is commonly said that illegal immigrants "do the jobs that Americans won't do"—jobs that are either too dangerous or too low-paying for American citizens. The federal government recognizes the symbiotic relationship between illegal aliens and American industry and generally does not strictly enforce laws against hiring undocumented immigrants. According to the *Wall Street Journal*, 10 to 12 million employees, or 8 percent of the U.S. workforce, are undocumented.

Critics contend that the hiring of illegal immigrants to perform cheap labor ultimately hurts the American taxpayer. As Richard Lamm, former governor of Colorado, observed, "It is not 'cheap labor.' It may be 'cheap' to those who pay the wages, but for the rest of us it is clearly 'subsidized' labor, as we taxpayers pick up the costs of education, health, and other municipal costs imposed by this workforce." A study released by the Center for Immigration Studies, an immigration research organization, stated, "Households headed by illegal immigrants imposed more than $26.3 billion in costs on the federal government in 2002 and paid only $16 billion in taxes, creating a net fiscal deficit of almost $10.4 billion, or $2,700 per illegal household." The same study also showed that illegal aliens imposed a burden on America's social programs, such as Medicaid and food assistance programs as well as the prison, court, and health care systems. In addition, some critics argue that the willingness of illegal immigrants to work for low wages displaces American workers and decreases pay for all workers.

The tension between the need for cheap labor and the impulse to protect American workers and taxpayers is among the subjects discussed in this chapter. Additional viewpoints further explore the costs and benefits of illegal immigration.

*"If immigration continues at 2.3 mil-
lion per year, we won't have enough
Americans to stand up for America."*

Illegal Immigration Threatens America

Frosty Wooldridge

*In the following viewpoint, Frosty Wooldridge contends that a
massive influx of illegal immigrants is creating social divisions
and undermining America's culture and economy. He argues
that these disruptions could lead to a civil war in America.
Wooldridge is a journalist and author whose articles and op-eds
have appeared in several newspapers and national and international magazines. He is the author of* Immigration's Unarmed
Invasion *(2004).*

As you read, consider the following questions:

1. What evidence does the author provide to support his
   view that America is breaking up?
2. How would granting amnesty to illegal immigrants per-
   petuate the immigration problem, according to Wooldridge?
3. In the author's view, why is the upcoming civil war going to start in California?

Have you ever noticed that it's 'we' average citizens who know what's going on long before politicians in high places get wind of it? Have you noticed more and more people speaking different languages at the supermarket? Schools? Movies? At your local bank? Have you noticed radio stations and TV crackling with Spanish or other languages in our English speaking America? Have you seen more people disrespecting the singing of our national anthem? Have you noticed our laws being broken such as red lights being run or people fleeing accident scenes where they were the cause? Have you noticed more trash in our state and national parks, especially in California, Texas and Georgia?

Have you noticed more flags being flown from other countries instead of Old Glory? Did you know that more Mexican flags fly from houses, cars and establishments in California more than the Stars and Stripes? Have you noticed what has happened to the Golden Bear State? Texas? Arizona? How about Georgia or Miami, Florida?

Have you ever been incredulous about hearing something that sounded so preposterous that it "couldn't be true"? Take a second look.

The Breakup of America

You are watching the "Coming Breakup of America." That's right. Your country. It is moving methodically, perversely, steadily and provocatively across our land. Our Congress is aiding it at the highest levels. It is a nation-destroying experiment being forced on America that will prove more disastrous than 9/11.

Last week [prior to July 7, 2004], I read a book, *Civil War Two: The Coming Breakup of America* by Thomas W. Chittum. This book paints a grim picture of what is happening to our country. At first, I was incredulous at his supposition. But halfway through the book, his research was so profound and SO evident that it became a page-turner. It provided a sickening look into the methodology and process whereby my own country was being destroyed before my eyes.

"History is littered with wars which everybody knew would never happen," said Enoch Powell. Today, America fights a war 10,000 miles away [in Iraq] while its own borders suffer an invasion so vast, so powerful, so insidiously destructive, yet so subtle—even our own citizens can't see it. Not yet, that is. Chittum writes, "America was born in blood." He should know because he is a decorated Viet Nam veteran.

"Social, political and economic forces are pulling America apart and driving her toward a bloody conflict that may fracture the nation into several different countries," he said. "Riots, gangs, militias, exploding crime rates, massive immigration, rising unemployment, falling wages . . . these fuel the fires of war."

Nations Versus Empires

He talks about nations versus empires. "Empires consist of peoples of different religions, languages, cultures, races and nationalities," he said. "Nations are dominated by one group that makes up a majority of the population. Nations are inherently stable while empires are always unstable."

If you look around the United States, we were a stable nation before 1965 with a population mostly of European and African citizens and mostly one religion. Today, we've imported 60 million people from areas so incompatible with American culture that we recoil at the horrors of female genital mutilation from Middle Easterners, polygamy of Hmong immigrants, honor killings from Asia, forced 13 year old girls into marriages and 300 different languages. Los Angeles, Miami, San Francisco and other cities speak more foreign languages than English. "If you'll notice throughout history," he writes, "multiethnic empires break up in cataclysmic violence." The former Soviet Union and Yugoslavia are classic examples

Illegal Immigration and Population Growth

Illegal immigration . . . contributes to the dramatic population growth overwhelming communities across America—crowding school classrooms, consuming already limited affordable housing, and increasing the strain on precious natural resources like water, energy, and forestland. The immigration authorities estimate that the population of illegal aliens is increasing by an estimated half million people annually.

Federation for American Immigration Reform, "Illegal Immigration Is a Crime," March 2005.

of multiethnic empires that shattered in tribal violence. Today, France is on the same track of self-destruction.

Chittum talks about an unstable, tiered society. Aristotle said, "The only stable state is the one in which all men are equal before the law." As any average American citizen can see, we're developing a massive underclass of illegal, Third World, uneducated poor that have become our 'indentured servants.' They won't remain down on the farm for long.

America supports 13 million illegal aliens that have no allegiance to our country. A dozen cities feature more foreign-born immigrants than American citizens. Last year [2003], 800,000 Californians fled their state. Over 200 Spanish-speaking radio stations own the airwaves in Los Angeles. Miami features over 100 Cuban stations. None have any allegiance to America.

The Problem of Amnesty

How will it get worse? Our politicians may grant amnesty to that 13 million which will encourage another 13 million.

There are so many illegal aliens that they hide more illegal aliens via 'ethnic sympathy.' But what they bring us is as dangerous as any armed invasion.

As their numbers grow, they are aided by the Mexican American Legal Defense and Education Fund. La Raza, another anti-American Mexican organization, works directly for the overthrow of America. LULAC is another group that supports the 'Reconquista of Aztlan,' or, the retaking of the American Southwest back into Mexico.

Notice that Mexican president [Vicente] Fox dictates to our leaders what they will do with his 13 million illegal immigrants in our country. Notice 46 Mexican consulates in our cities around America supporting his people in our country. Notice voter fraud by illegal aliens now able to throw our local and national elections.

After three chapters, Chittum's writing sobered me, but I still wasn't convinced until he offered concrete numbers. "In California in 1993, 665,229 firearms were sold. That's 1,873 per day. Enough firearms were sold to equip an infantry battalion." For the Californians remaining, there's a lot of frightened people readying themselves for conflict.

"California is odds-on favorite to kick off Civil War II," Chittum said.

Immigrant Gangs

"The instinctive need to be a member of a closely-knit group fighting for common ideals may grow so strong that it becomes inessential what these ideals are," said Konrad Lorenz. Illegal Mexican border jumpers separate against being an American. The 20,000 member "18th Street Gang" in Los Angeles owns the streets. They coordinate all drug traffic, extortions of businesses, prostitutes and robberies. Their power, along with MS-13 gangs in 28 American cities, grows by the day. Over 60 percent of the members are illegal aliens and the other 40 percent are legal immigrants. Since they possess no working skills in our First World society, they find crime as an easier vocation. It's termed 'Third World Momentum.' Its corruption is so deep, so wide and so embedded that it's as intrinsic as the sewer systems in those cities.

How many and how much? Los Angeles sheriff files register 100,000 gang members. San Antonio features 5,000 gang members. Chicago estimates 50,000 members. Former Attorney General Janet Reno estimated over 500,000 gang members have imported themselves into the USA. They commit an average of 580,000 crimes annually in our country.

So why do our politicians sit and twiddle their thumbs? Why do they aid and abet by doing nothing? Can't they see what's happening to California? Texas? Arizona? The answer in a nutshell: No!

Why? Because Americans, like the proverbial frog being thrown into the pot of water and the stove being turned up to high, will keep adapting until we boil to death. The same thing happened to the Romans, French, Spanish and every other great nation that tumbled into the dustbin of history. Spain backed into submission by the Madrid train bombing. France stands on the doorstep of a crisis it won't be able to contain.

I never thought I would have to fight for my own country inside my own country. But the time is fast approaching. Chittum adds that if immigration continues at 2.3 million per year, we won't have enough Americans to stand up for America.

> *"None of the claims made by conservatives to inveigh against immigration hold up to scrutiny."*

Illegal Immigration Does Not Threaten America

Tim Wise

Tim Wise is an activist and author of Great White Hoax: Responding to the Politics of White Nationalism. *In the following viewpoint he responds to several of the claims made by critics of immigration. Contrary to the assertions of these anti-immigration forces, he argues, illegal immigrants are not taking advantage of the welfare system and are not to blame for high rates of violent crime in American cities. Wise concludes that most of the arguments made by anti-immigration activists are based in racism.*

As you read, consider the following questions:

1. What evidence does the author present to show that the influx of illegal aliens has been exaggerated?
2. What flaws does the author identify in the study by Donald Huddle?
3. How does NAFTA contribute to the illegal immigration problem, according to Wise?

Tim Wise, "Defending the Unwelcome Stranger: The Truth About Immigration," *LIP Magazine,* September 26, 2004. Copyright © 2004 by *LIP Magazine.* Reproduced by permission of the publisher and author.

Before September 11, before the Patriot Act, before the latest round of racial profiling at airports, in which Arabs or those suspected of being Arab have been subjected to heightened scrutiny as potential terrorists, life was already difficult enough for immigrants of color to the United States.

In 1994, California voters approved Prop 187, the purpose of which had been to limit if not eliminate a wide array of income support, educational and health care benefits to so-called "illegal aliens." Although most of the law's provisions have been effectively blocked by the courts, the anti-immigrant backlash signified by the election result made clear that to be an immigrant to this country at this time was to be a suspect.

If not suspected of terrorism, being an immigrant was to be suspected of laziness, taking advantage of welfare programs, overburdening social services and health care facilities, lowering the quality of education with demands for bilingual instruction, or even worse, driving the drug trade and contributing heavily to the nation's crime problem.

But as with the overreaction to Arabs and Muslims so prevalent after September 11th, so too are the stereotypes, fears, and assumptions about immigrants from Latin America, the Caribbean, Africa and Asia false. When subjected to scrutiny, the reactionary ravings of white supremacist groups and even mainstream conservatives are shown to be wholly unsupported.

Exaggerated Claims

In this time of renewed Nativist impulses, perhaps we would do well to revisit some of the more traditional anti-immigrant rhetoric, so as to demonstrate the fallacies that permeate the discourse and restore some sanity, not to mention accuracy to the debate over this important issue.

To begin with, the supposed "alien invasion" has been greatly exaggerated. A recent study by demographers in the U.S. and Mexico City found that the numbers of illegal immigrants entering the U.S. is only about 105,000 per year, as opposed to the millions claimed by anti-immigrant forces.

Other estimates place the total number of undocumented entrants into the U.S. at no more than 300,000 annually—even then a far cry from the proclamations of anti-immigrant groups. What's more, the population of undocumented entrants into the U.S. has remained constant as a share of the national population for over two decades, at no more than two percent.

Myths About Immigrants, Welfare, and the Economy

As for immigrant use of welfare benefits, undocumented workers and their families are not eligible for cash welfare or food stamps. They are only eligible for emergency medical assistance, prenatal care and educational benefits, all of which are considered worth providing so as to reduce health emergencies, epidemics and the social problems associated with lack of schooling.

In fact, a proper analysis of welfare receipt rates shows that immigrants are not more likely than native-born residents to receive welfare. Excluding emergency refugees (who are eligible for several types of assistance in virtually any country to which they escape), recent immigrants receive public aid at lower rates than the native-born and immigrant use of welfare has been decreasing for over twenty years.

Contrary to common perception, today's immigrants (largely of color) are actually less likely to receive assistance than were the European immigrants of the early 1900s. Over half of all welfare recipients in 1909 were immigrants, and these immigrants were three times more likely to receive assistance than the native-born.

As for the cost of immigration to the public sector, rather than draining taxpayer coffers, immigrants actually contribute positively to the economic health of the United States; indeed,

A Nation of Immigrants

Immigration is not undermining the American experiment; it is an integral part of it. We are a nation of immigrants. Successive waves of immigrants have kept our country demographically young, enriched our culture and added to our productive capacity as a nation, enhancing our influence in the world.

Daniel T. Griswold, Insight on the News,
February 18, 2002.

recent immigrants create a net surplus to the public sector of nearly $30 billion annually, according to the Urban Institute.

Data from New York State—with the second largest immigrant population in the nation—shows that the foreign born population there pays about $18 billion in taxes each year, with a per capita tax payment that is hardly distinguishable from their native-born counterparts. Even those immigrants who are in New York illegally (only 16% of immigrants in the state) pay over $1 billion annually in taxes.

In California—home to 43% of illegal immigrants in the U.S.—undocumented workers contribute approximately seven percent of the state's economic product: roughly $63 billion annually. According to a study by researchers at UCLA, the gross economic contribution by each illegal immigrant to the economy of California was nearly $45,000 per year.

Given that the average undocumented worker receives very low wages—typically less than $10,000 annually—this means that even with paltry social service benefits available to these immigrants, the net transfer of income is exactly the opposite of that implied by immigrant bashers. Instead of the state and nation subsidizing immigrants, it is more accurate to say that immigrants subsidize the economy and the companies for which they work by performing low-wage labor that is worth at least four times more, on average, than what they earn from income and welfare combined.

A Flawed Study

The study most often cited to "prove" the high cost of immigrants relative to the taxes they pay was conducted by Donald Huddle, of Rice University, on behalf of the anti-immigration group, Carrying Capacity Network. Yet further analysis of the Huddle study by researchers at the Urban Institute revealed several flaws which undermine its conclusions.

While Huddle claimed that immigrants cost U.S. public coffers $42 billion annually, this number was arrived at through a terribly flawed methodology. First, Huddle was basing his claims on one study of Los Angeles County, which he then extrapolated to the nation as a whole, despite significant differences in the costs associated with immigration in different parts of the country, and the different incomes earned by immigrants across the nation. Indeed, Huddle's underestimation of immigrant income was so extreme, that he miscalculated the amount of taxes paid by these immigrants by roughly $21.3 billion.

Then, by ignoring altogether the FICA taxes (Social Security), unemployment insurance taxes, and gasoline taxes paid by immigrants, Huddle further underestimated the tax payments of immigrants by an additional $29 billion. These two mistakes alone (and there were others) torpedo Huddle's conclusion—that immigrants are a net drain on the nation's economy—by indicating that taxes paid by immigrants are higher than the amount they cost the country in public expenditures.

The Real Parasites

Of course there is a bitter irony in the claim that immigrants seek to take advantage of the U.S. welfare system; namely, if anything, it is U.S. corporations whose desire to take advantage of trade agreements and labor in exploited nations has led to the flow of immigrants to the U.S. in the first place.

For example, as a result of trade agreements that open up Mexico and Latin America for U.S. corporate penetration, companies have moved south of the border in search of low-wage labor and intent on developing markets for exports, especially in agriculture. As a result of the shift from local subsistence farming to profit-oriented corporate agriculture, Mexican peasants are driven off the land, at which time they head for Mexican cities in search of jobs. But the lack of jobs in the cities and large pool of unemployed labor there—which allows employers to drive down wages since workers are desperate—then results in a stream of workers from the Mexican cities into the United States.

Current research estimates that over 300,000 Mexican farm workers have lost their jobs due to NAFTA [the North American Free Trade Agreement], thereby fueling the desperate rush for the U.S. border in search of subsistence. In fact, if anyone is taking advantage or "sponging" off of others, it is the American corporations who run to Mexico where low wages and non-existent environmental laws allow them to save as much as $25,000 per worker compared to what they would have to pay in the United States.

Myths About Immigration and Crime

As for criminality, it appears that immigrants only pick up these bad habits after being in the country a while. A study at the University of North Carolina found that it is only after immigrant families become more "Americanized" that they experience dramatic increases in drug use, weapons use, violence and sexual promiscuity.

Indeed, Mexican immigrants have drug abuse rates that are only half as high as their U.S.-born, Mexican American counterparts, indicating that it is acculturation and Americanization, not immigration, which presents the larger problem. Studies have found that immigrants nearly always exhibit lower crime rates than native-born persons, and there is simply no evidence to indicate that as immigrants move into an area crime goes up.

Evidence from Miami—a large city with a substantial number and percentage of Latino and Caribbean immigrants, and the largest percentage of Latino residents of any large county in the U.S.—indicates how flawed the "immigration brings more crime" argument really is. Despite the city's large presence of immigrants, the fact remains that Cubans, Jamaicans, and Haitians are actually less likely to be involved in homicides than the native-born, and as the rate of Latino immigration to Miami increased in the 1980s, the murder rate there actually declined.

Haitian immigrants, in fact, typically commit murder less often than whites and have the lowest rate of homicides of any ethnic group in Miami. Likewise, there are no significant differences in the rates of homicides between Latinos and whites in Miami. While it is true that Miami led the nation in terms of its homicide rate throughout most of the 1980s, this was also the case in the late 1940s and early 1950s, long before the immigration explosion that would transform the town in more recent decades.

Dreaming of a White Nation

Ultimately, however, the battle over immigration is not about money, welfare programs, language or crime: it is about the desire by a large segment of the U.S. citizenry to define what it means to be an "American" in explicitly racial terms. Not only do such persons fail to recognize America as a continent, which includes the very dark-skinned neighbors to the South they so fear, but they also fail to conceive of the U.S. as anything less than a white nation.

Of course, such a racialized conception of the United States is intriguing, precisely because this country, unlike many others, has long been a multiracial, multicultural land, which would be unrecognizable as the nation it is today but for the contributions of people of color from distant and not so distant shores.

From the beginning of conquest and colonization of the Americas, the land that is now the U.S. was always multiracial. Not only were there millions of indigenous American Indians, representing over two hundred separate nations, but the numbers of African slaves often equaled or even surpassed the numbers of "free whites" in many communities, particularly in the south.

Until the massive increase in European immigration beginning in the mid-1800s and lasting until the 1920s, people of color were a substantial portion of the population in many communities as much as a third or more. Only by changing the inherent makeup of United States demography via "white" migration did the U.S. become 90% white in the 1950s.

In the final analysis, none of the claims made by conservatives to inveigh against immigration hold up to scrutiny: immigrants are no more and perhaps less likely to receive public assistance than the native-born, they are no more and often less likely to engage in serious criminal activity; and ultimately, their desire to live in the U.S.—especially given the anti-immigrant backlash of recent years—is testament to nothing so much as their desire to take advantage of the greater opportunities still available here, relative to the places from whence they come.

Of course, a few more years of Bushanomics might well remedy the situation: after all, if there aren't any jobs being created, no one will want to come to the United States.

> *"Illegals ... cost American taxpayers $10 billion every year in federal expenses alone!"*

Illegal Immigrants Harm America's Economy

S.J. Miller

In the following viewpoint S.J. Miller responds to various claims made by pro-immigration advocates. He rejects the argument that illegal aliens are necessary to the American economy and provide a source of cheap labor that is beneficial for American business. In fact, Miller asserts that illegal immigration is devastating the American economy. He believes that the American government is complicit in the problem by subsidizing the presence of illegal immigrants as a means to maintain a cheap labor force that can compete in the global economy. Miller is a writer focusing on trade and immigration issues.

As you read, consider the following questions:

1. How does the author respond to the claim that illegal immigrants pay taxes and Social Security contributions?
2. What economic sectors are supported by illegal immigration, according to Miller?
3. How can Americans save their country from the "global agenda," in the author's opinion?

S.J. Miller, "The U.S. Economy Will Collapse Without Illegal Alien Labor," *The Federal Observer*, 2005. Copyright © 2005 by *The Federal Observer*. Reproduced by permission.

Let's be clear about what this claim really means, if true: that the nation's economy depends on "cut-rate labor," requiring that we continue the outrage of illegal immigration despite all the widespread harm it does to Americans and our society.

We've heard this excuse before, long before anyone heard of "global economy" or the WTO [World Trade Organization]. American southerners claimed their economic survival depended on slave labor, even with tariffs applied to imported cotton, rice, indigo, and tobacco. Notice the same industry leads the insistence on today's illegal immigration: agriculture.

"Cheap labor," indeed. They might at least call slavery by its rightful name. Does anyone notice the irony that the liberals who opposed slavery in the 1850s are today advocating illegal immigration to deliver "slaves" to big business?

Taxes and Social Security

"They pay taxes."

The few pennies paid in sales tax on non-food purchases don't change an illegal alien into a person deserving the privileges of citizenship. The sales tax on his motel room and restaurant meals paid by Mohammed Atta (leader of the 9/11 terrorists) didn't make him a law-abiding, taxpaying American citizen. The same applies to other illegal aliens.

Precisely what other taxes do they pay? Certainly not federal or state income taxes; they claim enough dependents that their income tax withholding is zero. Moreover, they file federal tax returns only to claim the Earned Income Credit— given to taxpayers with children even if they don't owe income taxes!

"They pay into Social Security even though they will never collect benefits."

Q. How can that be since illegal aliens can't get a Social Security number?

Answer #1 They're using forged Social Security cards, stealing someone else's number. The increase in identity theft linked to illegal immigration was recently reported by MSNBC.

When I read that government officials have known of the problem for years but refuse to notify affected citizens, I wondered if that's the reason I receive an annual Earnings Statement (Form SSA 7705-SM-SI) that asks me to verify its accuracy, *and*

Answer #2 They pay Social Security taxes only if they have a "mainstream job" (defined as "a job Americans WILL do"). Here's another example of illegal alien advocates contradicting their own propaganda.

When confronted with the much higher rates of public assistance for immigrants vs. the native born, the return propaganda is:

"They may not contribute economically, but their contribution in cultural diversity makes up for it" and *"They are bringing their rich culture."*

Is this a cultural exchange or a "guest worker plan?" Why the attempt to deceive the public by misrepresenting a "guest worker plan" (or an amnesty) as a "cultural exchange program"?

Economic Harm

"Our economy would be devastated without them . . ." and *"They make a vital contribution to our economy."*

"They add much more to the economy than they take away" and *"They contribute more than they get (in return) . . ."*

The High Cost of Cheap Labor: Illegal Immigration and the Federal Budget by the Center for Immigration Studies [CIS] buried this nonsense for once and for all. Even considering Social Security "taxes" illegals pay by stealing another American's Social Security number, they still cost American taxpayers $10 billion every year in federal expenses alone! That doesn't include state expenses: education, medical care, welfare benefits (payments, housing, food stamps), jail costs, and higher insurance premiums for law-abiding citizens!

For years, studies from pro-immigration groups "proved" this by lumping legal immigrants and illegal aliens together. Because legal immigrants tend to be better educated with better paying jobs, their numbers concealed the negative economic "contribution" of the illegal aliens. That myth died with the CIS study.

And don't forget two additional "costs" the CIS study didn't mention:

1. $311 billion in uncollected taxes cited by the *Barrons* study.
2. $40 billion annually in remitted wages to home countries, according to the best source imaginable—Western Union.

Sustaining Lawyers

That illegal immigration and the presence of illegal aliens in the US enables and sustains certain economic sectors is undeniable. That said, what would be the loss should these two disappear entirely?

1. Immigration lawyers' groups who support every proposed illegal alien amnesty *and*
2. Non-profit and "church" groups using government (i.e. taxpayers') funds to provide "safety net assistance" for illegal aliens.

1) *Immigration lawyers.* Immigration lawyers are almost as dependent on illegal aliens as agriculture, although they won't admit it as openly. When Congress passes an amnesty, immigration lawyers do a land-office business. AILA (American Immigration Lawyers' Association) has full-time Congressional lobby teams to influence immigration policy to their benefit.

The AgJobs Amnesty program (S-1645, HR 3142) sponsored by Senator Larry Craig & Congressman Chris Cannon gave preferential treatment to applicants represented by attorneys. While pressure on 108th Congress was heavy for passage, the *Salt Lake Tribune* revealed that, after requiring applicants to use an attorney or designated entity for the application process, the AgJobs Amnesty then allowed the illegal alien access to public funds to pay the lawyers' fees. The reporter wrote that Cannon allowed immigration lawyers access to the "AgJobs" drafting process, as well as heavy contributions by non-Utah immigration lawyers to Cannon's campaign.

But Congressman Cannon and Senator Craig weren't alone in writing legislation to benefit immigration lawyers! The Jackpot Amnesty by Senator Ted Kennedy and Congressman Gutierrez (S-2381, HR-4262) also allowed illegal aliens to hire a lawyer to handle their amnesty at the expense of American taxpayers.

So get rid of the lawyers. That idea didn't originate with me, by the way; it's adapted from Mr. Shakespeare's *Henry VI* (Part 2, Act 4, Scene 2).

Supporting Non-Profits

2) *Non-profit "charities" receiving taxpayer funds.* "Charities" long ago stopped being agencies providing emergency help; they've now become part of the socialistic agenda for redistributing income. In our naive belief that US government agencies follow the "separation of church and state" forced on us by the ACLU [American Civil Liberties Union] and similar allies, we never consider that these "charities" are disguised government agencies. Yet talk to "career" employees of non-profit charities! You'll think you're dealing with a government employee, and for good reason—both groups operate with taxpayers' money. Like the immigration lawyers, they also use taxpayers' money to pay for federal and state legislative lobbyists to influence public lawmakers and policymakers.

More Services, Less Taxes

As the U.S. developed into a welfare state, poor illegal immigrants increasingly used a larger percentage of taxpayer dollars through reliance on government programs and use of other government resources, such as law enforcement and deportation. Further, since many U.S. employers illegally hire these workers at substandard wages, they avoid collecting social security taxes from them in order to hide their existence. This results in less taxes paid by illegal immigrants for the government services they disproportionately use.

Rachel Alexander, "Illegal Immigration
Solution Must Focus on Costs,"
OpinionEditorials.com, September 11, 2005.

The main difference is how their money is delivered. Government agencies receive money directly from government budgets, while "non-profits" receive their money largely from financial grants, largely hidden from public accountability.

They range from the two local groups below to nationals like Catholic Charities, USA, and even internationals. Most "government" money comes from grants out of White House Cabinet Departments: Dept of Labor, Health & Human Services, Education, Housing & Urban Development, and even Justice Dept!

They'd like us to believe they operate on voluntary donations, but the fact is that most depend heavily on government grants. Were they limited to voluntary donations to fund their "outreach" programs to illegal aliens (and others), I predict at least half would close. Remaining charitable activities would be severely curtailed.

Eliminate Parasitic Groups

That there's no public debate justifying continued taxpayers' subsidies to these groups is no surprise because the subsidies themselves are carefully kept VERY "low profile." But unlike most so-called "economic loss," elimination of these two parasitic groups would be a net gain to every American taxpayer.

Writing proposals for government grants is non-profit groups' bread and butter. College students majoring in government will complete at least one course in writing grant proposals from both government agencies and private foundations.

A "caught red-handed" example was recently exposed by Terry Graham of Colorado when she revealed that taxpayers' money and her state governor aided and abetted illegal aliens. Two "non-profit" groups operating with substantial government funding printed and distributed *"Enterese! (Inform Yourself), Survival Guide for Recent Arrivals to Colorado. "* Signed by Colorado governor Bill Owens, the booklet (paper and online) outlined how illegal aliens might obtain jobs, get free health care and seek low-cost attorneys.

Following the Money

"Following the money" (i.e. their tax documents) for Salud Family Health Centers and Focus Points Family Resources Center makes it undeniable: our government is providing money to "non-profit charities" who use that money to help illegal aliens obtain more "services and benefits" paid with taxpayers' money:

Focus Points Family Health Centers:

Total revenue of $431,835—56% from government grants

Plan de Salud del Valle (DBA Salud Family Health Centers):

Total revenue of $8,798,851—98.7% from government grants

These two are among many "non-profits/charities" who knowingly recycle American taxpayers' money into assistance to illegal aliens.

Volunteers during Arizona's Prop 200 campaign discovered another example when the Roman Catholic bishops publicly opposed Prop 200, even printing a "Vote NO on Prop 200" block in their parish newspaper *Catholic Vision.*

Catholic Community Services,
Southern AZ:
Government Grants & Match $18,219,543 (73.5% of annual budget)
Donations
Additional fees from immigration/ $4,025,853
adoption clients

Catholic Charities, Central &
Northern AZ:
Government Grants $19,334,196 (84.6% of annual budget)
Additional Govt Grants— $3,036,574
Immigration & Refugee
Additional fees from Immigration $638,150
& Adoption clients

The "Big 5" non-profit immigrant advocates consistently lobby for increases in refugee and legal immigrant numbers, just as military contractors lobby for increased defense spending.

Violating Federal Law

We know that one of two things is happening:

(1) The feds aren't aware that citizens' money provides assistance to illegal aliens and Congress will act promptly to investigate and stop it, prosecuting the groups violating the law, or

(2) The feds are aware that citizens' money provides assistance to illegal aliens and have done nothing to stop the outrage but refuse to prosecute the violators.

If #2 is true, aren't federal officials tolerating violations of their own laws by "aiding and abetting illegal aliens" (Title 8, United States Code, Chapter 12, subchapter II, Section 1324)? In the same way they refuse to prosecute immigration law violations?

So in stopping illegal immigration, we get the added bonus of eliminating both immigration lawyers as well as an entire "industry" of taxpayer-funded non-profit groups who promote a cause that 80%+ of "we the people" oppose. Doesn't that qualify as a "win-win"?

The "Global Economy"

It's hard to obtain an "official government" rationale and justification for taxpayers' funding of benefits and services to illegal aliens, because no one in government wants to address the direct question. Instead they evade the question with "we didn't know" excuses. The "non-profits/charities" have a different answer: "we don't want to alienate people who need help with the fear of deportation." Some even openly admit knowingly "aiding and abetting," such as Tom Ziemann, director of Catholic Charities in Glenwood Springs, CO. The "Western Slope" area of Colorado includes the ski resorts where illegal aliens' "cheap labor" is in great demand. Eliminating the "side assistance" with the high living costs of resort area, the "cheap labor" illegals might leave the area.

I'm convinced it's all part of the US government's balancing act in transitioning the US to a "global economy." Government officials' policy provides publicly-financed "corporate welfare" to keep just enough American businesses afloat despite their obvious inability to compete with businesses in "cheap production" countries. They also hinder enforcement of immigration laws for the same reason.

Who in his/her right mind would think American business will successfully compete with global manufacturers considering the imbedded expenses American prices and wages must support:

a. the US military to send anywhere in the world to protect global business interests.

b. international "giveaway" programs, both from the US and indirectly via the UN.

c. "non-profits" like the charities above and "one-world" groups like UN, NATO, SEATO, and the rest.

d. "corporate welfare" that shifts corporate tax responsibility to citizens.

e. government acquisition of private property to aid business agendas.

How long will the US government continue the balancing act? Until global business says they're satisfied with its acquisition of wealth at the expense of Americans? Considering that they likely agree with the late Duchess of Windsor's adage that "You can never be too rich or too thin," it won't happen so long as a single American citizen owns property or has a dollar beyond survival expenses.

Who Made the "Global Economy" Decision?

Certainly not Americans. Like "mass immigration" decisions of Congress since 1965, the "global economy" decision was made in private meeting rooms by people not elected by "we the people." In some cases, Americans wouldn't even recognize names of those dictating the policies that govern their lives. Once the decisions were made "in the dark of night," it was easy to convince US government officials to end public debate on important topics and exclude Americans' from knowledge of their political world.

Today's illegal immigration fiasco is only one example proving Americans have trusted their elected representatives far too long. We're being confronted with other nasty surprises that resulted from global business control of the political world; 9/11 was only one of many to come, and the Bush "guest worker amnesty" was another surprise. We'll soon be faced with resumption of the military draft, sending troops for additional "regime change," and FTAA [Free Trade Area of the Americas].

Were these issues presented by either of the 2004 Presidential candidates? Were they included on election platforms of either political party?

In saving our country from the "global" agenda (of which mass immigration is only one part), Americans should consider our own form of "regime change." By seeking political allies in new places rather than the traditional "Republican/ Democrat" arena, because these parties no longer serve Americans' interests.

> "The fast-growing undocumented
> population is coming to be seen as
> an untapped engine of growth."

Illegal Immigrants Do Not Harm America's Economy

Brian Grow et al.

In the following viewpoint Brian Grow and his colleagues argue that corporate America has recognized the economic power of the undocumented alien population, which is estimated to be 11 million people or more. Companies such as banks, insurers, credit card companies, phone carriers, and mortgage lenders have reached out to this fast-growing population. In the process, illegal immigrants have been drawn further into the economic mainstream, which could benefit the economy by fueling economic growth and increasing the share of taxes paid by immigrants. Brian Grow, Adrienne Carter, Roger O. Crockett, and Geri Smith are reporters for Business Week *magazine.*

As you read, consider the following questions:

1. According to the author, what effect are *matrícula consular* cards having on the ability of illegal aliens to do business in the United States?
2. How many new illegal immigrant consumers enter the U.S. economy each year, according to the authors?
3. What percentage of farm laborers are illegal immigrants, as reported by the authors?

Inez and Antonio Valenzuela are a marketer's dream. Young, upwardly mobile, and ready to spend on their growing family, the Los Angeles couple in many ways reflects the 42 million Hispanics in the U.S. Age 30 and 29, respectively, with two daughters, Esmeralda, 8, and Maria Luisa, 2 months, the duo puts in long hours, working 4 p.m. to 2 a.m., six days a week, at their bustling streetside taco trailer. From a small sidewalk stand less than two years ago, they built the business into a hot destination for hungry commuters. The Valenzuelas (not their real name) bring in revenue well above the U.S. household average of $43,000, making them a solidly middle-class family that any U.S. consumer-products company would love to reach.

But Inez and Antonio aren't your typical American consumers. They're undocumented immigrants who live and work in the U.S. illegally. When the couple, along with Esmeralda, crossed the Mexican border five years ago [in 2000], they had little money, no jobs, and lacked basic documents such as Social Security numbers. Guided by friends and family, the couple soon discovered how to navigate the increasingly above-ground world of illegal residency. At the local Mexican consulate, the Valenzuelas each signed up for an identification card known as a *matrícula consular* for which more than half the applicants are undocumented immigrants, according to the Pew Hispanic center, a Washington think tank. Scores of financial institutions now accept it for bank accounts, credit cards, and car loans. Next, they applied to the Internal Revenue Service for individual tax identification numbers (ITINS), allowing them to pay taxes like any U.S. citizen—and thereby to eventually get a home mortgage.

Today, companies large and small eagerly cater to the Valenzuelas—regardless of their status. In 2003 they paid $11,000 for a used Ford Motor Co. van plus $70,000 more for a gleaming new 30-foot trailer that now serves as headquarters and kitchen for their restaurant. A local car dealer gave them a loan for the van based only on Antonio's *matriculac-ard* and his Mexican driver's license. Verizon Communications Inc. also accepted his *matricula* when he signed up for cell-phone service. So did a Wells Fargo & Co. branch in the pre-dominantly Hispanic neighborhood in northeast Los Angeles where they live. Having a bank account allows them to pay bills by check and build up their savings. Their goal: to trade up from a one-bedroom rental to their own home. Eventually, they also hope to expand their business by buying several more trailers. *Matrícula* holders like the Valenzuelas are "bring-ing us all the money that has been under the mattress," says Wells Fargo branch manager Steven Contreraz.

Growth Engine

For more than two decades, America's illegal aliens have been the target of national attention—largely for negative reasons. Their growing numbers put downward pressure on U.S. wages and new demands on schools, hospitals, and other public ser-vices. Fears of heavier social burdens and higher tax bills have led citizens and local officials to object with renewed vigor to what many perceive as an unwanted invasion from Mexico and other countries, especially to newer destination states such as Alabama, Georgia, North Carolina, and Tennessee. Yet all the while, farms, hotels, restaurants, small manufacturers, and other employers have continued to hire the undocu-mented with little regard to the federal laws intended to stop them.

At the same time, though, the fast-growing undocumented population is coming to be seen as an untapped engine of growth. In the past several years, big U.S. consumer compa-nies—banks, insurers, mortgage lenders, credit-card outfits, phone carriers, and others—have decided that a market of 11 million or so potential customers is simply too big to ignore. It may be against the law for the Valenzuelas to be in the U.S.

Breen. © 2005 by Copley News Service. Reproduced by permission.

or for an employer to hire them, but there's nothing illegal about selling to them.

So with a wary eye on the heated political debate, business is targeting the Valenzuelas and millions of others who have entered the country illegally. Many companies do so more or less openly. Wells Fargo has half a million *matrícula* accounts, a majority of them, they acknowledge, opened by unauthorized aliens who lack regular residency or citizenship papers. At the Valenzuelas' branch, fully 80% of accounts are opened by *matrícula* holders. Blue Cross of California, whose parent, WellPoint Inc., is the nation's largest health insurer, sells health insurance to *matrícula* holders from company-staffed desks set up inside Mexican and Guatemalan consular offices in the U.S. Sprint Corp. accepts such an I.D. for cell-phone contracts.

Other companies, such as Kraft Foods Inc., won't discuss the status of their customers but explicitly target Hispanic newcomers—more than half of whom are estimated to enter the U.S. illegally, according to a new study by Pew. The consumer-products giant provides workbooks at local English-as-a-second-language classes that include instructions for using coupons for products such as Kraft's Capri Sun drinks in U.S. grocery stores. It also hosts bilingual sweepstake events in Hispanic neighborhoods. "We need to fish where the fish are," says Robert Simpson, Kraft's director of multicultural marketing. He calls part of the Hispanic audience he's trying to reach the "unacculturated," meaning people unfamiliar with American culture and customs.

Effect on Immigration Policy

The corporate Establishment's new hunger for the undocumenteds' business could have far-reaching implications for America's stance on immigration policy, which remains unresolved. Corporations are helping, essentially, to bring a huge chunk of the underground economy into the mainstream. By finding ways to treat illegals like any other consumers, companies are in effect legalizing—and legitimizing— millions of people who technically have no right to be in the U.S. It's even happening in mirror image, with some Mexican companies setting up programs to follow customers who move to the U.S. All this knits the U.S. and Mexico closer together, further blurring the border and population distinctions.

The economic impact could be significant. While most analysts peg the number of illegal immigrants at 10 million to 11 million, a recent study by Bear Stearns Asset Management concluded that data on housing permits, school enrollment, and foreign remittances suggests there could be as many as 20 million. Either way, experts agree that the undocumented, a majority of whom are Hispanic, are one of the nation's largest sources of population growth. They add 700,000 new consumers to the economy every year, more even than the 600,000 or so legal immigrants, according to Pew's new study. What's more, 84% of illegals are 18-to-44-year-olds, in their prime spending years, vs. 60% of legal residents. Corporate sales and profits will get a shot in the arm if more of them move out of the cash economy, put their money in banks, and take out credit cards, car loans, and home mortgages. U.S. gross national product could get a boost, too, since consumers with credit can spend more than those limited to cash.

More undocumented immigrants paying income and property taxes would help ease the taxpayer strain for the schools, health care, roads, and other services illegals use. Crime could decline, too. Wells Fargo pioneered acceptance of the *matrícula* in 2001 after the police department in Austin, Tex., asked local financial firms for help in preventing holdups of undocumented immigrants who, lacking I.D.s to open bank accounts, tend to carry wads of cash. "The market has found a way to capture those dollars," says Robert Justich, a senior managing director of Bear Stearns Asset Management and co-author of the recent report *The Underground Labor Force Is Rising to the Surface.*

The political implications are less clear-cut. Further integration of illegals into the U.S. could help President George W. Bush in his uphill struggle over the past two years to launch a guest worker program. His plan would provide a path to amnesty and full legalization for many unauthorized residents. Companies are taking a position similar to the President's, in effect saying: There's no point in pretending that millions of people aren't here, so let's find ways to deal with them. . . .

Dependent on Illegal Labor

Big U.S. companies' embrace of undocumenteds as consumers has intensified as it has become clear in recent years that—no matter how loudly the anti-immigration lobby complains— the U.S. isn't about to deport illegals en masse. The 1986 law forbidding their employment may still be on the books, but the feds have almost completely given up enforcing it. Instead, since September 11 [2001] they have focused on nabbing potential terrorists who might slip into the country illegally, according to a June [2005] report by the Government Accountability Office (GAO). Last year [2004], the U.S. Immigration & Customs Enforcement agency brought just three actions against companies for employing illegals, down from 417 in 1999, according to the GAO. And only 2,300 of the country's 5.6 million employers used a computer system in 2004 to check employee Social Security numbers.

Unafraid of penalties, some U.S. industries have become so dependent on illegal labor that a wholesale expulsion would be crippling. Illegal immigrants now comprise fully half of all farm laborers, up from 12% in 1990, according to a recent Labor Dept. survey. They're a quarter of workers in the meat and poultry industry, 24% of dishwashers, and 27% of drywall and ceiling tile installers, according to Pew senior research associate Jeffrey S. Passel. Last year [2004], more than 1 million of the nation's 2.5 million new jobs went to Hispanics, mostly recent immigrants, according to a separate study by Pew. With millions of illegals here to stay, "companies will definitely adapt to working with [them] because they're the fastest-growing marketplace," says Bear Stearns' Justich.

Illegals' importance to the U.S. economy is key to the country's often schizophrenic views toward them. Chronic complaints from taxpayers and workers aside, companies that hire or sell to the undocumented simply have too much at stake to allow a backlash to get out of hand. Even politicians who thunder about illegals have trouble sticking to their convictions.

Such was the case with Republican Congressman Tom Tancredo of Colorado, who says he may run for President in 2008 on a largely anti-immigration platform. One suggestion he made last year: a tax on the remittances foreigners send home as a way to recoup the education and health-care costs Tancredo chalks up to freeloading. But he quickly dropped the idea after an outcry from Denver-based First Data, whose

Western Union unit took in $1.1 billion last year from such money transfers. First Data Corp.'s political action committee and its chief executive, Charles T. Fote, each wrote $2,000 checks in support of Tancredo's opponent. Tancredo won re-election but has revised his plan: Rather than tax the individual transaction, he proposes reducing foreign aid by the amount of remittances that countries like Mexico receive from their citizens in the U.S.

The problem for critics of illegal immigration is that corporate efforts to sell to the undocumented weaves them ever more tightly into the fabric of American life. This pragmatic relationship may be anathema to immigration critics. But day by day, the undocumented in the U.S. are finding it ever easier to save and invest their hard-earned dollars.

"The compelling truth about the danger and devastation on America's southern border is crying out to be told."

Illegal Immigration Harms Border Communities

Phyllis Schlafly

In the following viewpoint Phyllis Schlafly describes the impact of illegal alien smuggling on border communities along the southwestern border of the United States. She urges greater law enforcement in those areas as well as a greater awareness across the country as to the devastation illegal immigration causes in the Southwest. Schlafly is recognized as a leading conservative voice and the founder and president of the Eagle Forum, a national organization of citizens interested in public policy. She has written twenty books on a variety of subjects ranging from feminism to education.

As you read, consider the following questions:

1. How many immigrants cross the border each night in Cochise County, as reported by the author?
2. How has President Bush's amnesty proposal affected illegal immigration, according to Schlafly?
3. How does illegal alien smuggling work in the Southwest, as described by the author?

The television news media bring us daily, graphic reports from Iraq, where valiant Americans are battling danger, death and destruction of property. So why don't we get coverage about similar dramatic and scary confrontations taking place on the U.S. border?

The compelling truth about the danger and devastation on America's southern border is crying out to be told. Americans need to hear from the likes of Erin Anderson, whose family homesteaded in Cochise County on the Arizona-Mexico border in the late 1880s.

Ms. Anderson says these American pioneers can't live on their own property any more because it's too dangerous. They can't ranch it. They can't sell it.

It isn't safe to go on their own property without a gun, a cell phone, and a two-way radio. Their land has been stolen from them by illegal aliens while public officials turn a deaf ear.

Cochise County in the Tucson sector is the major smuggling route for illegal aliens and drugs, and literally thousands cross every night. The Border Patrol admits to apprehending one out of five illegals, but many think it's only one out of ten.

The number of illegal aliens apprehended on the southern border jumped 25 percent in the first three months of 2004 compared with . . . [the previous] year. In Tucson the increase was 51 percent, in Yuma, it was 60 percent.

The news of President Bush's amnesty proposal spread like wildfire as far south as Brazil. After Border Patrol agents reported that the illegals said the amnesty proposal had prompted them to come, U.S. agents were told not to ask the question any more.

Trashing the Land

Ms. Anderson says that American landowners watch in horror as their lands, water troughs and tanks, and animals are de-

Catch and Release

Thousands on the fugitives list gave themselves up to Border Patrol agents shortly after crossing into the USA from Mexico to take advantage of a controversial "catch and release" policy that U.S. immigration officials have used because of crowded detention facilities along the Southwest border.

The policy allows a captured illegal immigrant to remain free in this country if the person agrees to appear at a court hearing, which often is scheduled in a U.S. city that was the immigrant's destination. But about 86% of those who agree to show up in court do not, and they become fugitives.

Knowing they're unlikely to be jailed, thousands of immigrants have surrendered to Border Patrol agents, then have been allowed to continue their journey into America, court summonses in hand.

Kevin Johnson, USA Today, *January 5, 2005.*

stroyed. The daily trampling of thousands of feet has beaten the ground into a hard pavement on which no grass will grow for the cattle.

Places that the illegals use as layover sites, where they rest or wait for the next ride, are littered with mountains of trash, garbage, open latrines, and plastic bags, diapers and wrappers of all kinds. When indigenous wildlife and cattle eat the plastic and refuse, they die, so the residents try to clean up the sites as often as they can.

The large number of discarded medicine wrappers indicates the prevalence of disease among the illegals. It is estimated that 10 percent of all illegals are carriers of Chagas, a potentially fatal disease that is widespread in Central America.

Sometimes the Americans who clean up the sites pick up pocket trash: scraps of paper with the name and phone number of the illegal alien's destination in the United States. This indicates that these border crossings are a very well organized migration.

Other suspicious items picked up by local residents include Muslim prayer rugs and notebooks written in both Arabic and Spanish. These items came from OTMs (Other Than Mexicans) and a subcategory called Special Interest Aliens, who are illegals coming from terrorist sponsoring countries.

The increased crime rate is frightening. Arizona has the highest rate of car theft in the nation, and residents risk home invasion and personal attacks.

The increase in violence is very intimidating to American residents. They are afraid to speak out because someone takes note of who they are and where they live, and gives that information to smuggler cartels in Mexico.

People Smuggling

People-smuggling by men known as coyotes has piggybacked on the already well established drug smuggling networks and infrastructure, and has become the third largest source of income for organized crime. Drug smuggling and human smuggling are now interchangeable.

Smuggling has become a recognized industry in Mexico. The smuggling route is very mechanized, and some northern Mexican villages have become known as smuggling industry towns.

Illegals fly or take a bus from anywhere in Mexico or Central America to an industry town like Altar in the northern region. They are driven to the Arizona border, walk a few miles across the border, and then are picked up by shuttle buses which take them north to Tucson or Phoenix.

Shuttle buses are common carriers, so they are not required to ask for citizenship ID as the airlines do. Often the coyotes take their passengers to stash houses in Phoenix and then hold them for ransom even though they have already paid their smuggling fee.

People smuggling is so lucrative and pervasive that it is corrupting some local American high school kids. Youngsters can make thousands of dollars a week by picking up illegal aliens on the road and driving them to the Phoenix airport.

When is the Bush Administration going to put troops on our southern border to stop these crimes, and when are the media going to interview Erin Anderson and other Arizonans so the American people can know what is really going on?

"We must stop the use of LIC [Low Intensity Conflict] along the border before this strategy spreads as a means by our government to repress opposition and maintain control."

Enforcement of Immigration Laws Harms Border Communities

Border Action Network

The Border Action Network is a grassroots membership organization that was formed to protect human rights, civil rights, and the Sonora desert along the Arizona-Mexico border. In the following viewpoint the organization contends that enforcement of the southwestern border of the United States has become excessively militarized. The use of military troops and equipment has led to an atmosphere of fear in the region and to human rights abuses against illegal immigrants.

As you read, consider the following questions:

1. What is low intensity conflict, as defined by the Border Action Network?

2. How has the war on drugs led to harsher treatment of immigrants, according to the author?

3. What examples of vigilante actions does Border Action Network cite?

Low Intensity Conflict (LIC) is a particularly insidious strategy of militarization that is specifically designed to deteriorate the quality of life in areas where it is used. The increasing militarization of the US-Mexico border with military troops, training and equipment as well as collaboration between the military and civilian law enforcement are a poignant example of low-intensity-conflict doctrine being used on US soil. A primary facet of the strategy is to purposely create a climate of fear, wherein people subjected to LIC are too afraid of the repressive government apparatus to resist it.

One of the primary means for creating this fear is human rights abuse, which is an integral part of LIC. In Latin America, LIC is civilian-targeted warfare, designed to remove support for guerrillas by targeting their support bases, people who live in areas where they are active, their civilian sympathizers. Such a strategy is being used along our border, as residents are made to fear those who cross (due to the war propaganda of dehumanizing and misleading rhetoric) as well as the security forces themselves, as they increasingly resemble an occupying force.

War Mentality

LIC consistently results in an increase in violence against women, including physical and sexual assaults and verbal abuse, as the foot soldiers of LIC engage in a campaign of terror with little accountability in the anything-goes, warlike atmosphere. Within a three month period of the fall of 2000, two cases merged where Border Patrol [B.P.] agents are accused of raping women. As in the past, however, agents are routinely not punished for their gross abuse of power.

Such abuse in not merely the result of insensitive, poorly trained personnel, although this certainly is a factor. Such abuse is an inherent part of LIC strategy, and part of the war mentality that is being propagated along the border. Everyone who crosses, or who may know or help someone else who crosses, is seen as the enemy, and treated accordingly.

LIC often results in massive environmental destruction, from manual and mechanical defoliation and destruction of habitat, to widespread use of chemical and biological agents. Along our border, sensitive riparian areas and endangered species habitats are being destroyed by massive road building and wall construction projects, the installation of cameras and stadium-style lighting, "off-roading" by B.P. agents and tire dragging to remove fragile desert vegetation. Low-level helicopter flights are disrupting critical bird migration patters and resulting in the separation of Sonoran pronghorn antelope fawns from their mothers. Only 150 Sonoran pronghorn antelope remain in the U.S.

As the military gains more control over border law enforcement, the war mentality begins to take precedence over solid law enforcement policy, as well as local governance. Federal military units, and militarized local law enforcement units, have less respect for the terrain, people and communities in which they work. Militaries are trained to kill, not protect and serve.

From the beginning, the militarization strategy along the border has been justified by the war on drugs, and from the beginning it has bled over into immigration enforcement. In the early 80's, interdiction techniques and technology, ostensibly deployed to detect drug smuggling have been used to track and detain migrants as well. This is very problematic in terms of respect for human and civil rights, as the vast majority of migrants crossing the border are not drug traffickers.

In fact, the vast majority of drug traffic passes through legal ports of entry, so the ongoing militarization and destruction of the border environment represents a complete misallocation of funds, at the very least—unless, of course, the real target is migrants, who have been forced out into the desert by Border Patrol strategy.

The Tide of Vigilantism

The tide of armed vigilantism has risen in Arizona, adding heat and hatred to the desert state, while doing nothing to solve legitimate problems. Whether proclaiming an imminent loss of American "culture" due to immigration or organizing armed patrols to hunt humans, these anti-immigration extremists have deliberately confused border control policy with intolerance and paramilitary activity. They promote a culture of lawlessness and defiance that will only add to, not solve, America's border problems.

Los Angeles Daily News, *"Extremists at Border," May 16, 2005.*

Vigilantism

LIC has consistently employed the tactic of creating armed paramilitary groups that work in collaboration with government security forces to further the propagation of fear. These groups operate with impunity as they engage in human rights abuses on behalf of security forces, which are afforded a measure of deniability for the worst transgressions of their policy. We are seeing this along our border, with vigilante groups violating people's human and civil rights with total impunity. Migrants are routinely round up at gun point and detained by vigilante groups. Migrants have also been found dead in the desert with gunshot wounds and one migrant was found with rope marks around his neck. To date, local, state, and national law enforcement agencies have refused to prosecute any of the openly unlawful and abusive vigilante actions.

In Latin America, elite intelligence units have often ended up targeting those who oppose the government on any grounds, whether or not they have anything at all todo with guerrillas. In the drug wars along our border, it was already stated policy to develop and share intelligence among various agencies, even if it overlaps into immigration enforcement. After September 11th, this intelligence sharing policy was extended to include law enforcement agencies throughout the United States. How long before this intelligence capability is used to target groups opposing U.S. policies?

The use of low-intensity conflict is a strategy used by governments to instill fear in their citizenry as a means of repression. The United States use of this strategy within its borders and against its citizens is an increasingly disturbing trend with far-reaching implications. We must stop the use of LIC along the border before this strategy spreads as a means by our government to repress opposition and maintain control.

Periodical Bibliography

The following articles have been selected to supplement the diverse views presented in this chapter.

Robert J. Caldwell   "Common Sense on Immigration," *San Diego Union-Tribune*, April 24, 2005.

Layne Cameron   "The Frontlines of Illegal Immigration," *American Legion*, March 2001.

Madeleine Pelner Cosman   "Illegal Aliens and American Medicine," *Journal of the American Physicians and Surgeons*, Spring 2005.

Jon Dougherty   "The Immigrant 'Cheap Labor' Myth," May 27, 2005. www.worldnetdaily.com.

James Flanigan   "Immigrants Benefit U.S. Economy Now as Ever," *Los Angeles Times*, July 3, 2005.

Brian Grow   "A Massive Economic Development Boom," *Business Week*, July 18, 2005.

Diana Hull   "U.S. Can't Ignore Toll of Illegal Immigration," *Detroit Free Press*, June 30, 2005.

Greg James   "A Pragmatic Approach to Illegal Immigration," *Seattle Times*, June 17, 2005.

Sue Kirchhoff and Barbara Hagenbaugh   "Immigration: A Fiscal Boon or Financial Strain?" *USA Today*, January 22, 2004.

Charles Krauthammer   "Assimilation Now," *Washington Post*, June 17, 2005.

Claudine LoMonaco   "Push Is on for Faster Immigration," *Tucson Citizen*, July 4, 2005.

Edwin S. Rubenstein   "Illegals and the Economy," February 5, 2004. www.vdare.com.

Phyllis Schlafly   "Illegal Immigrants from Mexico Pose Real Threat to Social Security," November 15, 2004. www.townhall.com.

Irwin M. Stelzer   "Immigration in the New Economy," *Public Interest*, Fall 2000.

OPPOSING
VIEWPOINTS®
SERIES

CHAPTER 2

Does the United States Treat Illegal Immigrants Fairly?

Chapter Preface

Illegal aliens face a number of hardships to migrate to and survive in the United States. In order to cross the border, they often experience dangerous and expensive border crossings. Once in the country, many labor under dangerous conditions for substandard pay with insufficient legal and economic protections. Others may face antiforeigner discrimination. Because of their tenuous legal position and their social isolation resulting from language and cultural differences, they feel they have little recourse other than to work under such circumstances.

Since the terrorist attacks of September 11, 2001, illegal immigrants have been faced with additional obstacles. Immigration laws were reformed to more closely monitor the borders. In some cases the FBI picked up illegal aliens in sweeping raids and detained them for months without charging them or giving them due process of law. "In the wake of the devastating terrorist attacks of September 11, we all feel vulnerable in ways that we have never felt before, and many have argued that we may need to sacrifice our liberty in order to purchase security," argues David Cole, a professor of constitutional law at Georgetown University Law Center. "In fact, however, what we have done is to sacrifice the liberties of some—immigrants, and especially Arab and Muslim immigrants—for the purported security of the rest of us."

While views on immigration vary widely, most people agree that immigrants should be afforded basic human rights. However, more debate exists on the degree of legal protection and civil liberties to which illegal immigrants are entitled. Some contend that illegal immigrants who work and make positive contributions to the economy and culture deserve minimum wages, driver's licenses, and voting rights. Others insist that by violating the law to enter and remain in the country, illegal immigrants have revoked their right to many legal protections and privileges.

Opinions about what degree of legal protections undocumented immigrants are entitled to range from none at all to the full benefits of citizenship. This question is among the issues addressed in the following chapter.

> "One tragic consequence of the [Border Patrol's] suppression policy has been to divert migration flows from a few traditional, urban crossing points to more scattered rural areas—to the ... deadly peril of migrants."

Border Patrol Efforts Cause Illegal Immigrant Deaths

Daniel Griswold

Daniel Griswold is the associate director of the Center for Trade Policy at the Cato Institute, a libertarian public policy research center. He has written frequently on the subject of trade and immigration. In the following viewpoint he maintains that the Border Patrol's enforcement efforts endanger the lives of illegal aliens crossing the southwestern border. Because the Border Patrol has intensified its control of the most heavily traveled areas, illegal immigrants have been forced to cross the border in more isolated rural areas in which they risk dying of exposure to extreme heat.

As you read, consider the following questions:

1. What percentage of illegal immigrants in the United States come from Mexico, according to Griswold?
2. How many U.S. jobs will require only short-term training by 2010, as reported by the author?

3. In the author's view, how would creating a legal path for Mexican laborers to come to the United States improve national security?

The 11 Mexican migrants found dead in a sealed rail car in Iowa [in October 2002] ... were twice victimized—directly by smugglers who callously left them to die, and indirectly by a U.S. immigration law in conflict with the realities of American life.

While the U.S. government has encouraged closer trade, investment, and political ties with Mexico, it has labored in vain to restrict the flow of labor across the border. Starting with the clampdown on illegal immigration in the mid-1980s, the U.S. government has imposed new and burdensome regulations on American employers and dramatically increased spending on border control. Despite those aggressive efforts, America's border policy has failed to stem the flow of undocumented workers into the U.S. labor market.

Diverted Migration Flows

Today 8 million people live in the U.S. without legal documents, and each year the number grows by an estimated 250,000 as more enter illegally or overstay their visas. More than half of the illegal immigrants entering and already here come from Mexico.

One tragic consequence of the suppression policy has been to divert migration flows from a few traditional, urban crossing points to more scattered rural areas—to the frustration of rural residents and the deadly peril of migrants. Before the crackdown, the large majority of Mexican migrants entered via three narrow, urban gates—San Diego, Calif., and El Paso and Laredo, Texas. In response to the beefed-up border enforcement begun by the Clinton administration in 1993, migration patterns shifted to remote rural areas such as the

Arizona-Mexico border where patrols are more scattered but conditions are also more dangerous.

The diverted flow has caused headaches for Americans living in those areas as migrants have trespassed on private property, disturbed livestock, and destroyed property. But the consequences have been deadly for more than 2,000 migrants who have perished since 1995 from heat and dehydration in remote areas of the desert or in sealed trucks and rail cars.

Economic Reality

America's immigration laws are colliding with economic reality, and reality is winning. Migration from Mexico is driven by a fundamental mismatch between a rising demand for low-skilled labor in the U.S. and a shrinking domestic supply of workers willing to fill those jobs. The Labor Department estimates that the total number of jobs in our economy that require only short-term training will increase from 53.2 million in 2000 to 60.9 million by 2010, a net increase of 7.7 million.

Meanwhile, the supply of American workers willing to do such work continues to fall because of an aging workforce and rising education levels. By 2010, the median age of American workers will reach 40.6 years, while the share of adult native-born men without a high school diploma continues to plunge: from more than half in 1960 to less than 10% today. Older, educated Americans understandably have better things to do with their work time than to wash windows, wait tables and hang drywall.

Create a Legal Path

Mexican migrants provide a ready source of labor to fill that growing gap. Yet immigration law contains virtually no legal channel through which low-skilled immigrant workers can enter the country to meet demand. The result, predictably, is illegal immigration and all the black-market pathologies that come with it.

Doing the Nation's Most Dangerous Jobs

More than 6,800 Hispanic workers died on the job from 1992 through 2001, new government employment and Census data show. Their workplace fatality rate jumped 15.1% in that period, even though the rate fell 15.4% for all other workers.

Many were Mexican immigrants with poor English skills. They took the only jobs they could get. They were often repaid with death. Poisoned by toxic fumes. Crushed by falling equipment. Burned alive.

They died, in part, because they took some of the nation's most dangerous, thus hard-to-fill, jobs in construction and factories, government data show. They were often too scared of losing jobs to press for safer working conditions, advocates say. There weren't enough government inspectors to help ensure their safety, and lax penalties failed to discourage safety-law violators. Although lawmakers, regulators and prosecutors are stepping up efforts to reverse the trend, labor advocates worry it may take a major disaster—such as the 1911 Triangle Shirtwaist Factory fire that killed 146 immigrants, later spurring workplace reform—before real change is made.

Jim Hopkins, USA Today, *March 13, 2003.*

Progress toward fixing the problem of illegal migration was derailed by September 11, but most members of Congress understand that Mexican migration is not a threat to national security. The Enhanced Border Security and Visa Entry Reform Act of 2002 ... represents the right kind of policy response to terrorism. The law focuses on identifying terrorist suspects abroad and keeping them out of the U.S. Notably absent from the bill were any provisions rolling back levels of legal immigration or cracking down on undocumented migration from Mexico.

Indeed, creating a legal path for the movement of workers across the U.S.-Mexican border would enhance national security. It would begin to drain the swamp of smuggling and document fraud that facilitates illegal immigration, and would encourage millions of currently undocumented workers to make themselves known to authorities by registering with the government, reducing cover for terrorists who manage to enter and overstay their visas.

Legalization would allow the government to devote more resources to keeping terrorists out of the country. Before Sept. 11, the government had stationed more than four times as many border enforcement agents on the Mexican border as along the Canadian one, even though the Canadian border is more than twice as long and has been the preferred border of entry for Middle Easterners trying to enter the U.S. illegally. A system that allows Mexican workers to enter the U.S. legally would free up thousands of government personnel and save an estimated $3 billion a year—resources that would then be available to fight terrorism....

President Bush and President [Vicente] Fox ... should reaffirm their earlier commitment to make migration across the border "safe, orderly, legal and dignified." Such a system should include a new temporary worker visa that would allow Mexican workers to enter the U.S. labor market legally for a certain period, and allow undocumented workers already in the U.S. to earn legal status based on years of work and other productive behavior.

Current immigration law has made lawbreakers out of millions of hard-working, otherwise law-abiding people—immigrant workers and native employers alike—whose only "crime" is a desire to work together in our market economy for mutual advantage. Death in a boxcar is perverse punishment for seeking a better life.

> "These deaths are not 'caused' by law enforcement or by [Border Patrol] efforts such as Gatekeeper and Hold the Line; the Border Patrol and the INS have been the scapegoats."

Border Patrol Efforts Do Not Cause Illegal Immigrant Deaths

Peter K. Nunez

In the following viewpoint Peter K. Nunez rebuts the charge that stringent Border Control enforcement has led to the deaths of illegal immigrants. Rather, he contents that the deaths of immigrants attempting to cross the border illegally are ultimately caused by government policies in Mexico and the United States. In Mexico, conditions that keep citizens poor push migrants to seek a better life in America. In the United States, policies that reward illegal immigrants with social services provide incentive to poor Mexicans to migrate. Policies in both Mexico and the United States must be changed in order to curtail the flow of immigrants and reduce the number of tragic deaths. Nunez is the chairman of the board of directors at the Center for Immigration Studies, an organization that seeks limits on immigration to the United States.

As you read, consider the following questions:

Peter K. Nunez, testimony before the U.S. House Subcommittee on Immigration, Border Security, and Claims, Committee on the Judiciary, Washington, D.C., June 24, 2003.

1. What immigration policy reforms are necessary, according to Nunez?

2. By what percentage did the number of illegal immigrant deportations decrease between 2001 and 2002, as reported by Nunez?

3. What social services are available to illegal immigrants, as stated by the author?

The tragic deaths involving the truck in Victoria, Texas, [in May 2003] once again demonstrate the deadly consequences arising from the complete failure of our current immigration policy to deal with the chaos along our borders resulting from illegal immigration. . . .

Unfortunately, deaths along the border related to illegal alien smuggling are not a new phenomenon. It was not at all unusual for people to die trying to enter this country along our southern border during the sixteen years I served as a federal prosecutor in San Diego. Deaths due to exposure to the elements, to traffic accidents, and to the inhumane treatment received from smugglers were all too common even during the '70's and '80's. It has always been a matter of the highest priority for both the Border Patrol and the U.S. Attorneys offices along the border to investigate and prosecute cases where a death was involved. And I am aware of the extraordinary efforts that have been made over the past ten years—since the inception of Operation Gatekeeper in San Diego and Hold the Line in El Paso—by agencies of both the United States and Mexican governments, to warn would-be illegal aliens of the potential dangers they faced in trying to cross the border illegally through the deserts and mountains.

Notwithstanding these efforts, deaths have continued to occur, and will continue as long as we fail to control our borders and as long as we cling to an outdated, failed, and disastrous immigration policy. Because if we try to find the cause of these deaths, and if we are trying to prevent them, then we need look no further then to the unwillingness of the United States to reform its immigration laws in light of the realities of the 21st Century.

"Push" and "Pull" Factors

Clearly criminal responsibility for these deaths can be laid at the feet of the smugglers who left these poor people to die in the back of a truck. It can also be argued that the illegal aliens themselves are partly responsible for their own deaths, given their willingness to risk harm by entering this country illegally, in violation of our criminal laws. But the illegal aliens who attempt to enter this country by putting their lives at risk, and the smugglers who feed off the desperation of these people, are all reacting to a set of circumstances that act as both "push" and "pull" factors in stimulating the flow of immigrants from Mexico and the Third World to the United States. The plain fact is that the huge disparity in economic conditions between Mexico and the United States, as well as the abundant social services available to immigrants once they arrive here, will compel people to attempt the journey even in the face of danger and hardship.

So until Mexico is willing and able to deal with the "push" factors that force millions of its citizens to seek a better life in the United Sates, and until the United States is willing to deal with the "pull" factors that lure millions of poor people here from around the world, we should expect that deaths among immigrants will continue to occur. These deaths are not "caused" by law enforcement or by efforts such as Gatekeeper and Hold the Line; the Border Patrol and the INS [Immigration and Naturalization Service] have been the scapegoats, told to enforce the law, but not given the resources needed to do the job correctly. What we need to do, at least along the border, is to expand Gatekeeper and Hold the Line to those trouble spots that now represent the biggest threats of illegal entry. Just as the Border Patrol was doubled in size during the early and mid-'90's to provide the resources needed in San Diego and El Paso, now we must add however many more Border Patrol agents needed to close the remaining gaps.

Eliminate Incentives

But "border control" alone will never be enough. What is needed is a comprehensive reform of our immigration policy designed to eliminate all of the perverse incentives that continue to draw illegal aliens to this country. If it is true that most immigrants—both legal and illegal—come to this country to work, then it is essential to finally enact an employer sanctions provision that works. Equally important, however, is the need to reestablish an effective interior enforcement mechanism designed to locate, arrest, and deport the 8 million-plus illegal aliens now living in the United States. For nothing works as a better incentive for illegal aliens than the fact that they know that no one will bother them if they are able to reach the interior of the United States.

Beginning in the late 1980's, INS began retreating from their historical and statutory mandate to locate, arrest, and deport those illegal aliens who managed to evade the Border Patrol or INS inspectors at our ports of entry, and those non-immigrants who originally entered legally but who overstayed their visas. This abdication of the interior enforcement function escalated during the '90's, and has all but disappeared in the current environment. Only the horrors of 9/11 have resulted in any effective interior enforcement, and that is aimed solely at potential terrorists.

In fact, while the latest INS figures show a 75% increase in the deportation of Arabs and Muslims (FY 2002 compared to FY 2001), the same figures show an OVERALL DECREASE of 16% in the total number of deportations. In FY 2002, 28,833 fewer deportations took place than the preceding year; the biggest decline was among Mexicans, the single largest national group, which saw a decline of 32,692 illegal alien Mexicans.

So if you were a poor Mexican living in Mexico, you would know that your chances of being caught crossing the border would be slight, and even if you were caught, nothing bad would happen to you. There would be no prosecution, and no other meaningful sanction to dissuade you from attempting to enter illegally. And you would also know that once you made it past the Border Patrol, you would essentially be home free, that no one would be looking for you after you arrived at your destination in the interior of the United States. And you would know that there would be jobs available for you, even if you might be cheated by your employer, that there would be some level of free medical care for you and your family, free public education for your children, and perhaps even some additional benefits for you and yours, all at the expense of the American taxpayer. . . .

Deaths Caused by Illegal Aliens

One last point about deaths relating to illegal immigration. We should be as concerned about the deaths (and other violent crimes) caused BY illegal aliens as we are about the deaths of illegal aliens that occur during the course of their own volitional acts of illegally entering this country.

On June 13 of this year [2003], Oceanside Police Department officer Tony Zeppetella, age 27, was gunned down and executed by one Adrian Camacho, described as "an Oceanside gang member with a history of violence and drugs." (*San Diego Union-Tribune*, June 20, 2003) What the news article does not report is that the defendant has been convicted on numerous felonies, and has previously been deported as an illegal alien! Too bad the Oceanside Police Department and the San Diego County Sheriff's Office were not interested in illegal aliens. Too bad that the INS in San Diego does not have an effective program designed to locate, arrest, and deport illegal aliens. Maybe if they did, Officer Zeppetella's widow and

Wright. © by Copley News Service. Reproduced by permission.

six-month-old child would not be suffering today over their loss.

Or take the recent case from Northern California involving the kidnapping (and who knows what else) of a 9-year-old girl, who, thankfully, survived her ordeal. Her kidnapper? Another illegal alien, who was able to hide in plain sight, due in part to the policy of the San Jose Police Department to look the other way with regard to immigration violators. And of course the INS has no program to fulfill its statutory duty to locate, arrest, and deport illegal aliens.

So as we mourn the deaths of those who voluntarily decided to break our criminal law by entering this country illegally, let's also save a little compassion for those who become the victims of illegal aliens, with the full complicity of the federal government and state and local law enforcement agencies that have decided to look the other way.

The bottom line is that this Congress has to end the chaos of our past and present immigration policy, and put in place serious reform efforts that will enhance the ability of the new

INS to do its job. We must, as a country, stop sending a mixed message to the downtrodden of the world that we will leave you alone if you have the courage and the ingenuity to make it past our borders. The federal government must use all of its resources to attack this problem comprehensively. The state and local governments must be brought into the effort, and any and all incentives dangled by state and local governments must be ended. Only by turning off the magnets that provoke this lawlessness can we ever stop the chaos at the borders that results, unfortunately, in the loss of life.

> *"In one wealthy country after another, there has been an 'anti-immigrant backlash.'"*

Opposition to Illegal Immigration Is Based on Racism

Emile Schepers

Emile Schepers is a political activist and writer. In the following viewpoint, he contends that an anti-immigration backlash rooted in antiforeign racism is sweeping across the United States. Schepers identifies several anti-immigration organizations and questions their motives for opposing undocumented workers. He compares the anti-immigration movement in America to that of Europe and suggests that racism is the common cause of such sentiment.

As you read, consider the following questions:

1. According to the author, how have corporate globalization and NAFTA affected world immigration?

2. What is the solution to the poor treatment of undocumented workers, in Schepers's opinion?

3. How does the author respond to the charge that immigrants are polluting U.S. culture?

Emile Schepers, "Harvesting Hatred: Anti-Immigrant Racism Today,"*Political Affairs,* March 22, 2005. Copyright © 2005 by *Political Affairs.* Reproduced by permission.

A recurring theme in US history has been periodic anti-foreign frenzy. We are now in the throes of one of these episodes, with Mexican and other Latin American immigrants being portrayed by the ultra right as the most terrifying "alien" threat since H.G. Wells' *War of the Worlds.*

This comes at a moment when immigration is at an unprecedentedly high level not only in the United States, but all over the planet. Corporate globalization has penetrated the farthest reaches of the world, disrupting existing economic arrangements, driving farmers off their land and into already overcrowded cities, and creating conditions of ever more desperate poverty in Latin America, Africa, much of Asia and the former socialist states of Eastern Europe.

Country after country has been pressured by the World Bank and the IMF [International Monetary Fund] to implement economic measures that have left large sections of their populations unemployed and destitute. NAFTA [North American Free Trade Agreement] is estimated to have driven six million Mexican farmers and their relatives off the land since 1994. The powerful have insisted on trade policies that allow capital to go wherever it will generate more profit. But there has not been a parallel change in the rules regulating the movement of labor. Circumstances force tens of millions to try to emigrate, but they are not allowed to do so legally. Having no choice, they do so anyway.

Anti-Immigration Backlash

In one wealthy country after another, there has been an "anti-immigrant backlash." Even European countries heretofore famous for their tolerance of outsiders have banged the door shut, or are talking about doing so. Anti-immigrant movements and organizations have arisen in all the wealthier countries. Spectacles of fascist skinheads beating up immigrants or torching homes thought to harbor foreign-born people have become commonplace.

The Emergence of a New Racism

Once, the West saw its superior civilisation and economic system as under threat from the communist world. That was the ideological enemy as seen from the US; that was the hostile intransigent neighbour as seen from western Europe. Today, the threat posed by 125 million displaced people, living either temporarily or permanently outside their countries of origin, has replaced that which was posed by communism. For, in this brave new post–Cold War world, the enemy is not so much ideology as poverty. As western security agencies, supranational global bodies, intergovernmental agencies and national governments mobilise against migratory movements from 'overpopulated' and 'socially insecure countries with weaker economies', a whole new anti-refugee discourse has emerged in popular culture. Those seeking asylum are demonised as bogus, as illegal immigrants and economic migrants scrounging at capital's gate and threatening capital's culture. And it is this demonisation of the people that the capitalist western world seeks to exclude—in the name of the preservation of economic prosperity and national identity—that signals the emergence of a new racism.

Liz Fekete, Independent Race and Refugee News, *September 28, 2001.*

In the United States, the current anti-immigrant rampage comes from the same sources that support the Bush administration, and the initiation of the Iraq war. These same forces attack affirmative action, social welfare and democratic rights. This anti-immigrant movement cloaks itself in a suspect concern for the well being of US-born workers.

A whole network of organizations are specifically dedicated to immigrant-bashing. Among them are the Federation for American Immigration Reform (FAIR). FAIR fights for restrictive immigration policies and sealing the US-Mexico border. The Center for Immigration Studies is another outfit that puts out reams of reports and specializes in testifying at hearings to the effect that current immigration levels represent a threat to US culture, the environment, the economy or even the physical survival of country.

The organization which launched Proposition 200 in Arizona, an initiative to stop immigrants from getting driver licenses, Protect Arizona Now, is now trying to go nationwide. In Congress, some 71 House members, almost all Republicans, have formed an anti-immigrant caucus under the leadership of Tom Tancredo (R-Colorado), and are determined not only to pass extreme anti-immigrant legislation, but to block even President Bush's totally inadequate guest worker program.

Job Competition?

The anti-immigrant juggernaut has both ideological and practical dimensions. The ideological attack focuses on Mexican immigrants. Basing themselves on seemingly plausible statistics, anti-immigrant activists assert that immigrants compete for jobs with African Americans and other poor and minority sectors of the working class. Well-meaning people who are sympathetic to immigrants sometimes counter by saying that "immigrants only take jobs that Americans don't want." But this defense is limited. It is easily countered by the anti-immigrant response "well if immigrants were not so readily available and easily exploitable, those employers would have to make the jobs more attractive by cleaning up the workplace and offering better pay."

The fact is employers hire the undocumented precisely because they can pay them less, prevent them from unionizing and get rid of them when better pay is demanded. However, the solution is not to try to deport immigrants (which will weaken their position even more), but to allow them to organize and fight for better wages and working conditions. If the eight to 12 million undocumented immigrants currently thought to be in the United States were all deported, what would one have accomplished? In the world of corporate globalization, "competition" from desperately poor workers in foreign countries is a much more powerful tool for dragging down wages than is "competition" from immigrants. If all undocumented immigrants from Mexico currently working in the US would be "rounded up" (a racist phrase if ever there was one) and "sent back," it would cause a significant drop in wages in Mexico, which would make Mexico an even more attractive place for capitalists to move production.

Environmental Damage

A novel twist in racist anti-immigrant propaganda is to portray immigrants as a threat to the environment. This refers not only to things like littering on desert pathways immigrants use to enter the United States, but to the issue of "overpopulation" as well. The littering on the border would not happen if there were an orderly mechanism of labor movement. And the United States is not "overpopulated." In fact, most of the countries which send immigrants are much more densely populated than is the United States. This has not prevented anti-immigrant agitators from trying to use sectors of the environmentalist movement, such as the Sierra Club, as mechanisms to promote their anti-foreign agenda.

Relatively new is the tendency to blame Mexican immigrants specifically for the crisis in health care and health insurance coverage in the United States. Steve Camarota of the Center for Immigration Studies points out, correctly, that a large portion of the uninsured working poor are immigrants, especially Mexicans and other Latinos. Why poor immigrant workers don't have health insurance is no mystery: employers can get away with denying them on-the-job health coverage, and with paying them too little to afford to purchase family policies, because immigrant workers are vulnerable to employer reprisals when they demand better wages and benefits.

However, Camarota gives the impression that these immigrants somehow brought "lack of health insurance" with them in their suitcases when they came from Mexico. If they were legalized and allowed to become citizens, they would be less vulnerable and more able to fight for better conditions both in the workplace and the community.

Particularly obscene is the notion that immigrants are polluting US culture and threatening the English language. This is the central thesis of Samuel P. Huntington's book *Who Are We: The Challenge to America's National Identity.* Huntington asserts that the United States was founded by white Anglo-Saxon Protestants who imparted certain cultural values particular to their background to nation building. Latino immigrants can't adapt and thus damage the United States. In his scholarly way, Huntington expresses the old know-nothing anti-foreign position. Most people who make this claim cannot specify just what these special white Anglo-Saxon Protestant cultural values are that are so essential to democracy and lacking in foreigners. But if it means an adherence to democracy and freedom, this characteristic is at a very high level in most immigrant populations. And while first generation immigrants may struggle with English, their children almost always speak it as fluently as do other English speaking Americans. So this argument boils down to simple nativist bigotry.

> *"People who say it's racist to want se-*
> *cure borders are insulting the intelli-*
> *gence of the American people."*

Opposition to Illegal Immigration Is Not Based on Racism

Tom Tancredo

In the following viewpoint Tom Tancredo rejects the charge that it is racist to advocate protecting America's borders from illegal immigration and the possible influx of dangerous terrorists. He suggests that accusations of racism are merely attempts to discredit reasonable proposals for immigration policy reforms and increased border security. Tancredo represents Colorado's Sixth District in the U.S. House of Representatives and serves as the chairman of the Congressional Immigration Reform Caucus.

As you read, consider the following questions:

1. What is the REAL ID program, as described by Tancredo?

2. What are some recent successes by the immigration reform movement, according to the author?

3. How many non-Mexican citizens were caught illegally crossing the U.S.-Mexico border in 2004, as reported by Tancredo?

People who say it's racist to want secure borders are insulting the intelligence of the American people, and such charges betray an empty arsenal of serious arguments. No wonder the immigration reform movement is gaining on every front.

Last November's [2004] election gave momentum to the movement in a way not widely reported in the media but very much understood by political analysts and lawmakers. President Bush increased his share of the Latino vote from about 32% to 40% in that election—without using the immigration issue. A *New York Times* analysis of the Bush-Cheney campaign ads aimed at Latinos revealed that the issues used to attract Latino voters were economic empowerment, educational opportunity and traditional moral values. Not a single Bush-Cheney campaign ad mentioned Bush's guest-worker proposal or liberalized immigration rules.

Immigration Reform Victories

I predict that the immigration reform movement is about to score a monumental victory in Congress with the impending passage of "Real ID," a measure that will, among other things, set federal standards for driver's license documents and prohibit states from giving driver's licenses to anyone in this country illegally. The House passed these provisions in February [2005], and Senate Minority Leader Harry Reid (D-Nev.) has indicated that he thinks Democrats in the Senate will accept them as part of the defense supplemental appropriations bill.

This victory for border security and immigration control has its roots in the 9/11 commission report, but political events since election day 2004 have also played a large role. The 9/11 commission recommended the denial of driver's licenses to illegal aliens and better security for driver's license documents. Those provisions were passed by the House by a wide margin in October. Then on Nov. 2, a political earthquake occurred when Arizona voters approved Proposition 200, which denies state welfare benefits to illegal aliens and strengthens voter registration requirements. Forty-seven percent of Latino voters and 59% of Latino Republicans voted for Proposition 200.

These figures have liberated Republicans to speak candidly about immigration control without fearing the "race card." Opponents will still try to use it, but it rings hollow. In the words of Lyndon B. Johnson, "That dog won't hunt."

Genuine Border Security Needed

All of which means that Bush must have some other reason for continuing to push his ill-conceived proposal for amnesty for illegal aliens and for turning a blind eye to the dangers of open borders. He appears to be pandering not to Latino voters but to the government of Mexico. Is he so influenced by the corporate advocates for cheap labor that he cannot see the loss of millions of jobs by Latino and black Americans to the unfair competition of illegal labor?

There is now a broad consensus in Congress that border security must be given a high priority. We cannot think seriously about legalizing millions of new "temporary workers" until we are able to control our borders and know who is entering our country and who is leaving.

In 2004, there were more than 70,000 non-Mexicans caught trying to enter the U.S.—through Mexico! They came from Brazil, Syria, Pakistan, Indonesia, Iraq, China and 120 other countries, the Department of Homeland Security reports. What is wrong with the United States placing at least the same importance on border security as Mexico does in guarding its southern border with Guatemala and Belize? Mexico's love affair with open borders is selective; it applies only to the U.S. Does this selectivity have anything to do with the estimated $16 billion sent home to Mexico last year [2004] by Mexican nationals living in the U.S.?

A Special Dilemma

Unlike those immigrants that have preceded them, Mexican immigrants pose a special dilemma to this country. Due to geography, Mexicans, unlike the Irish of yesterday, do not have to cut ties with the nation they left behind. Because of the close proximity of Mexico and America, Mexicans need not be worried with assimilation to the American way of life. . . .

The battle over immigration is not about xenophobia or racism; such are just red herrings offered to distract from the real issue. The battle over immigration is about country, family and heritage.

Joe Murray, "La Reconquista,"
OpinionEditorials.com, May 23, 2005.

We can have genuine border security without jeopardizing legal trade and commerce with our neighbors. But there is some commerce we need to interrupt—the commerce in human smuggling, in drug smuggling and the export of criminal gangs to American cities. More than 10% of the inmates in U.S. jails and prisons are illegal aliens, and in California it is more than 20%. In 2002, 33.6% of criminals sentenced in federal district courts were noncitizens.

Last year in Los Angeles County, more than 30,000 criminal aliens who served jail sentences were released back into the community instead of being deported. What is the justification for this absurdity? Who will speak for the future victims of these criminals? Who dares call it racist to want these predators and 100,000 other criminal aliens at large across our nation sent home and kept away from our communities by secure borders?

Last month's [April 2005] Minuteman [a citizens' border-control group] protest on the Arizona border is only a harbinger of what is to come if political leaders do not take notice of legitimate citizen outrage over these absurdities. Citizens are demanding two simple things—border security and immigration law enforcement. When did law enforcement become a radical idea?

> "The group that has borne the brunt of
> the Bush administration's post-9/11
> crackdown is immigrants."

The War on Terror Victimizes Illegal Immigrants

Rachel Meeropol

Following the September 11, 2001, terrorist attacks on America, the Bush administration took measures to improve the nation's ability to prevent terrorists from entering the country illegally and to deport potential terrorists living in the United States. In the following viewpoint Rachel Meeropol maintains that these efforts have been excessive and have violated the civil liberties of illegal immigrants by subjecting them to roundups, detentions, and deportations. Meeropol is an attorney at the Center for Constitutional Rights and vice president of the New York City chapter of the National Lawyers Guild.

As you read, consider the following questions:

1. From the author's perspective, who was Farouk Abdel-Muhti and why is his story important?
2. What was the National Security Entry/Exit Registration System, according to Meeropol, and how did it violate the rights of immigrants?
3. How has the Illegal Immigration Reform and Immigrant

Responsibility Act led to harsh treatment of illegal immigrants, as reported by the author?

I first met Farouk Abdel-Muhti, on February 5, 2003 in a dingy visiting cubicle at Passaic County Jail in Paterson, New Jersey. At that point, he had already spent ten months in immigration detention. He was arrested in April of 2002 on a seven-year-old deportation order as part of the increasingly aggressive and targeted enforcement of civil immigration laws in the wake of 9/11. Farouk was a stateless Palestinian; he was born in Ramallah in 1947 and moved to New York in the seventies. The FBI and the INS [Immigration and Naturalization Service] had nowhere to send him, so like so many other immigration detainees without a home country, Farouk was simply placed in detention.

In many ways, Farouk's story follows that of . . . other post-9/11 detainees. . . . He was kept in the same overcrowded and brutal jails and faced the same physical and verbal abuse as was documented on video and in a report by the Office of the Inspector General. Like other post-9/11 detainees, Farouk was beaten repeatedly, harassed by guards, and constantly moved between facilities in New York, New Jersey, and Pennsylvania. In other ways, he was different from many other prisoners—shortly after I met with him, he was put in solitary confinement for eight continuous months in an attempt to prevent him from organizing other detainees against their detention and its brutal conditions. Even within these extremely restrictive surroundings, he still managed to educate and organize detainees *and* guards about social justice issues—such as reasons to oppose the U.S. war on Iraq.

Sentenced to an Early Death

Farouk was also different than most of the other noncitizens swept up in the U.S. government's aggressive post-9/11 policing in that he was eventually released and permitted to stay in the United States. In 2001, the Supreme Court ruled that if after six months in detention it is unlikely the government will successfully deport a person, that person must be released. In April of 2004, upon the orders of a federal court judge relying on that precedent, the Department of Homeland Security's Bureau of Immigration and Customs Enforcement (ICE) finally released Farouk.

Three months after he was released from prison, Farouk addressed the Philadelphia Ethical Society on the issue of "Detentions and Torture: Building Resistance." Immediately after giving his speech, Farouk died. He used his last breaths for his people. Those who knew Farouk believe that by illegally holding him in immigration detention where he was beaten, harassed, and denied proper medical care for over two years, ICE compromised his health and perhaps sentenced him to an early death. Those of us who worked with him were deeply shocked by Farouk's death—perhaps this is because Farouk never took the time to complain about his own problems, he was too focused on those of others. Notes from our interviews with Farouk over the past few years document his countless references to the medical and legal needs of other detainees, but only passing reference to his own inability to obtain the high blood pressure medication he needed. . . .

In the wake of the torture scandal at Abu Ghraib, and the lawless detentions at Guantánamo, it is all too easy to overlook a case like Farouk's. Yet the two years that were stolen from him are irretrievable, and the tragedy of his early and perhaps avoidable death is a stark reminder of the human costs of the Bush administration's response to 9/11. . . .

The Bush administration has reacted to the 9/11 attacks with policies, regulations, and rhetoric designed to scare the American public into accepting a full-fledged assault on civil liberties. This assault did not happen overnight; instead, the Bush administration built on oppressive laws and policies already in existence to consolidate executive and law enforce-

Open Season on Immigrants

The United States has changed. Since the 9/11 attacks, the endemic hatred of immigrants that has always infected this country has become paranoid. Every immigrant, in the minds of many Americans and especially public officials, has become a potential terrorist. Therefore it is open season on them to the bureaucrats in Homeland Security. Every new immigrant scalp they can gather means more points for their career advancement. Every immigrant family they can break up is another victory for American freedom.

Andrew Greeley, Chicago Sun-Times, *June 10, 2005.*

ment power through an erosion of our civil rights, and a campaign of intimidation, isolation, and profiling aimed primarily at activists, noncitizens, and immigrants of color. The Bush administration's actions post-9/11 cannot be misunderstood as a spontaneous eruption of repressive policies; rather, they represent a long-planned and well-developed move toward authoritarian control. . . .

Targeting Immigrants

The group that has borne the brunt of the Bush administration's post-9/11 crackdown is immigrants and noncitizens of color. Bush's racial profiling and overly aggressive policing of noncitizens has torn families apart and in many urban areas, destroyed whole communities. In Midwood and Brighton Beach, Brooklyn, for example, the *New York Times* reported that in the two years after 9/11, the Pakistani community shrank from 120,000 to half that. While the post-9/11 sweeps . . . are perhaps the most startling and egregious example of the morally repugnant (and startlingly inefficient) policy of using immigration status as a proxy for potential terrorists, the sweeps are not the entire story.

After a decade of progress in combating racial profiling in criminal law enforcement, the events of 9/11 have led to a wholesale resurgence of discriminatory official policy. For example, on September 11, 2002, the Immigration and Naturalization Services (INS) initiated the National Security Entry/ Exit Registration System (NSEERS), which required all male nonimmigrants over the age of 16 from designated countries to report to the INS to be questioned, fingerprinted, and photographed. Of the first 20 countries to be designated, all but one—North Korea—were Arab or Muslim. During the registration process, thousands of noncitizens were mistreated and detained unnecessarily, and now face deportation. In December of 2002, for example, the INS office in Los Angeles detained around 400 men—most of whom were Iranian or Iraqi exiles with minor visa violations—who went there voluntarily in order to register under NSEERS. These mass arrests led to many individuals becoming fearful of showing up to register, even when they had a valid immigration status. [Former attorney general John] Ashcroft has failed to explain how a *voluntary* requirement, which alienates the very communities in which law enforcement officials most need to build trust, could possibly help locate terrorists.

The INS (and later the Department of Homeland Security) responded to accusations of racial, ethnic, and religious profiling and discrimination by stating that it intended to eventually register all nonimmigrants. Instead, on December 1, 2003, the INS suspended yearly registration requirements amid massive public outcry against the discriminatory, haphazard, and intimidating way the program was being applied. Before the suspension went into effect, however, more than 82,000 men from twenty countries voluntarily came forward to comply with the time-consuming and invasive interviews, and more than 2,870 were detained for some period of time as a result. Although most of NSEERS's requirements have been suspended, those individuals who complied with the discriminatory law and were thus placed into deportation proceedings have received no clemency. Indeed, at least 2,000 men from New York, and over 13,000 nationwide face deportation today.

Harsh Laws

NSEERS was not the only new immigration requirement that blatantly relied on racial, religious, and national origin profiling. On December 5, 2001, the INS announced its new "Alien Absconder Apprehension Initiative," which provided the FBI with the names of 314,000 immigrants with outstanding deportation orders for inclusion in the National Crime Information Center database. The Department of Justice decided to initially focus on 6,000 of these individuals who came from countries with suspected ties to al Qaeda. Immigration violations are largely civil violations, not punishable by criminal law. Including such information on a criminal database means that a routine traffic stop can result in serious immigration consequences, and that police departments become responsible for enforcing the immigration laws.

Although racial profiling of noncitizens has become something of a pet project for the Bush administration, it is important to realize that many of the recent detentions and policies were made possible by racist immigration laws passed during the Clinton administration. In 1996, Congress passed and Clinton signed the Illegal Immigration Reform and Immigrant Responsibility Act, or IIRAIRA, which increased immigration officers' presence at borders and increased criminal penalties for immigration violations. The act allows, and in some cases requires, long-term detention of individuals who are awaiting a determination of their immigration status. The act expanded the definition of "aggravated felony" (crimes for which noncitizens can be deported) to include almost every felony, including things like shoplifting and other nonviolent, relatively minor offenses. Most of the noncitizens detained and deported under this harsh law before *and after* 9/11 were individuals of Caribbean and Latin American descent. The harshness with which these individuals are treated allows the Bush administration to brag of its get-tough policies and reassure the public of our impenetrable borders. There is no mention of the human toll, nor any way to quantify claimed increases in safety. . . .

Freedom Sacrificed for Nothing

If the voluntary special registration program failed to ferret out terrorist immigrants, and the post-9/11 special-interest detentions resulted in many deportations but no terrorism charges, why should we believe that the Guantánamo detentions and brutal interrogations at Abu Ghraib were any more effectively designed or executed? Taken together, we can see that the Bush administration's post-9/11 crackdown on civil liberties is not a story of freedom sacrificed for security, but of freedom sacrificed for nothing, or at least nothing useful. The deportations and detentions, alternately spun to the media as proof of our victories against terrorists or evidence of the continued threat, are nothing more than public relations stunts, purchased at a cost dear to the American people, and to people of color around the world.

| "Our southern borders remain open channels not only for illegal aliens and smugglers, but for terrorists."

Stricter Immigration Policy Is Essential to the War on Terror

Michelle Malkin

In the following viewpoint, Michelle Malkin claims that America's immigration and entrance system has failed to protect American citizens from terrorists, especially along the U.S.-Mexican border. She claims that by failing to enforce border laws, America is stuck in a pre-9/11 mind-set and remains vulnerable to another devastating terrorist attack. Malkin is a political commentator and syndicated columnist and has written books on immigration and terrorism.

As you read, consider the following questions:

1. According to the Immigration and Naturalization Service, how many illegal aliens from terror-friendly countries reside in the United States?

2. How have ethnic advocacy groups reacted to the immigration issue, according to Malkin?

3. What point does the author make by telling the story of Kris Eggle?

The voice of New Americans who reject political correctness and the cult of multiculturalism has been sorely missing from the debate on immigration policy. September 11 helped shatter that silence. . . . I've heard from countless readers, first- and second-generation Americans like myself and my family, who reject open borders and immigration anarchy. We are sick and tired of watching our government allow illegal line-jumpers, killers, and America-haters to flood our gates and threaten our safety. We are sick and tired of watching ethnic minority leaders cry "racism" whenever Congress attempts to shore up our borders. And we are especially sick and tired of business leaders, lobbyists, and lawmakers from both major parties caving in, forsaking leadership—and selling out our national security.

A year-and-a half after September 11 [2001], we have new laws, new agencies, and lots of new government spending to fight off foreign invaders. But our immigration policies leave the door to our nation open wide to the world's law-breakers and evildoers.

A Broken System

According to the Immigration and Naturalization Service, at least 78,000 illegal aliens from terror-supporting or terror-friendly countries live in the U.S. They are among an estimated seven to eleven million illegal aliens who have crossed our borders illegally, overstayed visas illegally, jumped ship illegally and evaded deportation orders illegally.

More than 300,000 illegal alien fugitives, including 6,000 from the Middle East, remain on the loose despite deportation orders.

Last year [2002], at least 105 foreign nationals suspected of terrorist involvement received U.S. visas because of lapses in a new background check system.

There is still no systematic tracking of criminal alien felons across the country.

The Threat of Terrorism Is from Illegal Aliens

The criminals who were convicted of the 1993 World Trade Center bombing, of the murders in front of the CIA headquarters in 1993, and who were involved in a 1998 plot to bomb New York's subway system were Middle East aliens who should not have been in the United States. They were either granted a visa that should never have been issued or had overstayed a visa and should have been expelled. The 1996 Khobar Towers bombings, the 1998 attacks on the U.S. embassies in Kenya and Tanzania and the 2000 attack on the USS *Cole* in Yemen were all carried out by radical Middle East groups.

Since easy access into the United States has been repeatedly exploited by aliens bent on terrorism, it should have been no surprise that it was used by the World Trade Center/Pentagon hijackers.

The policy of opening our borders to anyone who wants to sneak into our country illegally—or to remain illegally after entering legally—must be exposed and terminated. This is the most important security precaution our government must take.

Phyllis Schlafly, Phyllis Schlafly Report, *October 2001.*

Sanctuary for illegal aliens remains the policy in almost every major metropolis.

And "catch and release" remains standard operating procedure for untold thousands of illegal aliens who pass through the fingers of federal immigration authorities every day.

My book, *Invasion,* argues in great detail that our current immigration and entrance system is in shambles, partly by neglect, partly by design. From America's negligent consular offices overseas, to our porous air, land, and sea ports of entry, to our ineffective detention and deportation policies, our federal immigration authorities have failed at every level to protect our borders and preserve our sovereignty.

As the daughter of legal immigrants from the Philippines, I have never taken for granted the rights and responsibilities that come with citizenship. The oath my parents took—in English—when they were naturalized resonated even more powerfully with me after September 11:

"I hereby declare, on oath, that I absolutely and entirely renounce and abjure all allegiance and fidelity to any foreign prince, potentate, state, or sovereignty of whom or which I have heretofore been a subject or citizen; that I will support and defend the Constitution and laws of the United States of America against all enemies, foreign and domestic; that I will bear true faith and allegiance to the same; that I will bear arms on behalf of the United States when required by the law; that I will perform noncombatant service in the armed forces of the United States when required by the law; that I will perform work of national importance under civilian direction when required by the law; and that I take this obligation freely without any mental reservation or purpose of evasion; so help me God."

Ethnic Complainers

Patriotism surged after the September 11 attacks, but not among some ethnic advocacy groups. Hyphenated leaders who favor lax immigration policies characterized attempts to protect our borders from all enemies, foreign and domestic, as an unnecessary "backlash": Arab-American leaders complained that Arab-Americans were being singled out by the feds, Hispanic leaders complained that Hispanics were being singled out by the feds, etc. Meanwhile, at American airports, grandmothers and Medal of Honor recipients actually were being pulled aside and singled out by the feds.

These ethnic complainers were joined by profit-driven immigration lawyers, university officials and corporate executives, as well as vote-driven political strategists in both major parties, who refused to put the national interest above their own narrow interests. Contrary to their misguided claims, the demand for a more discriminating immigration policy—one that welcomes American Dreamers and bars American Destroyers—does not stem from fear or hatred of foreigners, but from self-preservation and love of country.

An Undeclared War

Last fall [2002], I met a wonderful family from Cadillac, Michigan. Bonnie and Bob Eggle brought their daughter Jennifer, along with several cousins, aunts, uncles, and a family friend, to the nation's capital. But the Eggles were not in Washington, D.C., on a sightseeing tour. Bonnie and Bob traveled to the Beltway because their only son, Kris, was killed over the summer along the U.S.-Mexico border by gun-toting Mexican drug dealers. The Eggles came to town to get someone—anyone—in official Washington to pay attention to the war no one wants to talk about these days: the War On America's Borders.

Kris worked as a U.S. Park Service Ranger at Organ Pipe National Monument in southern Arizona, which is considered one of the most dangerous federal parks in the nation. As many as 1,000 illegal aliens a day trample across Organ Pipe—trashing our fences, mining the environment, breaking our laws and endangering lives. It's a smugglers' paradise and a national security nightmare.

"We have caught people from China, Pakistan and Yemen coming through," says Bo Stone, an Organ Pipe ranger and close friend of Eggle. "If 1,000 illegal immigrants can walk through the desert here, so can 1,000 terrorists."

Some 200,000 illegal border-crossers and 700,000 pounds of drugs were intercepted at Organ Pipe last year [2002] alone.

According to Border Patrol agents, foreign invaders are so brazen that they've actually cleared their own private roads through the park. On August 9, 2002, Kris Eggle joined Border Patrol agents in pursuit of armed Mexican bandits. During the chase, he was ambushed. An Eagle Scout, high school valedictorian, champion cross-country runner in college and All-American guy, he was cut down by a sniper hidden in the desert brush with an AK-47. He took a bullet just below his protective vest and died on a dirt path before medics arrived. The Eggles celebrated Kris's 29th birthday at his hometown gravesite.

Inadequate Fences

In his spare time, Kris's father used to volunteer to help fix the fences along our southern border near where his son worked. "It is obscene," Bob Eggle told me, "how little our government cares about protecting the border." Referring to a century-old family farm in northern Michigan, Bob noted, "The worst cow fence on our farm is better than the best fences at the border."

Nor is Kris Eggle's murder an isolated incident. Several shootouts in the Southwest have occurred since last April [2002] some even involving incursions by Mexican military officers suspected of collaborating with criminal drug dealers. Just last week [February 2003], a Border Patrol agent was stoned in the head along the Tucson sector by a gang of illegal border-crossers. And again—as Kris's friend and fellow park ranger Bo Stone also points out—our southern borders remain open channels not only for illegal aliens and smugglers, but for terrorists.

The story is the same on the northern border, where a few months ago two reporters for the *Toronto Star* illegally crossed a dozen easy entry points between the boundaries that separate Quebec from Vermont and New York. Mangled fences and battered stop signs spraypainted with "U.S.A." are all that stand in the way. In Washington State, Montana and North Dakota, broken cameras and orange rubber cones are often the only objects that guard against intrusion. Yet calls for increased border patrol resources, park ranger staffing and military help have been ignored in Washington, D.C.

Unnecessary Deaths

Kris Eggle's murder in August 2002 came just weeks before my book, *Invasion,* hit the shelves. But his death is like so many of the deaths of innocent Americans I document in the book and in subsequent columns—brutal, tragic, unnecessary and undeniably linked to our federal government's systemic refusal to enforce immigration laws:

Six people died and thousands were wounded in the 1993 World Trade Center bombing at the hands of illegal aliens from Palestine, Egypt, Jordan, and Pakistan who freely overstayed their visas and exploited our loophole-ridden asylum system.

Twelve people died from 1997 to 1999 at the hands of illegal alien serial killer Angel Resendiz, who traipsed back and forth freely across the U.S.-Mexican border.

Five law enforcement officers, from Virginia to California, were gunned down in cold blood by illegal border-crossers and visa-violators whom the INS failed to apprehend and deport.

Three thousand people died on September 11, 2001, at the hands of 19 al-Qaeda terrorists who slipped past our snoozing State Department and INS. Five of the terrorist hijackers had freely overstayed student, tourist and business visas.

Last fall [2002], ten people died at the hands of sniper suspects John Muhammad and Lee Malvo. Muhammad had been stopped in Miami for attempted smuggling of illegal aliens, but was never prosecuted. Malvo was himself an illegal alien from Jamaica who had been apprehended by Border Patrol agents in Washington State, but then released pending deportation against Border Patrol recommendation.

In the aftermath of September 11, many advocates of unrestricted immigration on both the left and the right remain stuck in a pre-war mentality. They continue to argue that there is no connection between controlling illegal immigration and protecting national security. This unrepentant "open borders" crowd ranges from liberal Democrats Tom Daschle and Dick Gephardt, to the conservative *Wall Street Journal* editorial page and certain Bush administration officials. They consider it "scapegoating" to link lax immigration enforcement to September 11, and hold to the fatally flawed belief that we can allow millions of "good" illegal immigrants to stream across the borders while retaining the ability to screen out "bad" illegal immigrants who are seeking to destroy us.

Periodical Bibliography

The following articles have been selected to supplement the diverse views presented in this chapter.

Leslie Berestein   "Enforcement Is Focused on Border, Not Business," *San Diego Union-Tribune*, November 7, 2004.

Peter Brimelow   "'Racism'? Or Treason?" June 29, 2001. www.vdare.com.

Tom DeWeese   "How to Stop the Flow of Illegal Aliens," March 11, 2005. www.chronwatch.com.

John Florez   "Huntsman Should Confront Fox on Illegal Immigration," *Deseret News*, July 4, 2005.

Jim Hopkins   "Fatality Rates Increase for Hispanic Workers," *USA Today*, March 13, 2003.

Kathryn Jean Lopez with Michelle Malkin   "What Would Mohammad (Atta) Do?" *National Review Online*, September 18, 2002. www.nationalreview.com.

Michelle Malkin   "Ashcroft vs. the Chicken Littles," *Jewish World Review*, April 30, 2003.

Michelle Malkin   "The Illegal Alien Pander-Lympics," *Capitalism Magazine*, February 18, 2002.

Ira Mehlman   "The Issue Is Immigration," *National Review*, November 29, 2003.

John O'Sullivan   "See No Evil: Illegal Aliens and the Specter of Another 9/11," *National Review*, December 27, 2004.

Gabriel Thompson   "In Quest for Living Wage, Many Immigrants Make Ultimate Sacrifice," *New Standard*, February 4, 2005.

OPPOSING
VIEWPOINTS®
SERIES

CHAPTER 3

How Should America Enforce Its Borders?

Chapter Preface

Many lawmakers and concerned citizens argue that controlling the nation's borders is essential to America's national security and economic well-being. They contend that the inflow of illegal immigrants—especially across the southern border—could allow the entry of terrorists and could overwhelm the public services of border states like Arizona, Texas, and California. In response, they call for stricter immigration laws and beefed up border enforcement. Recommendations from these activists range from adding more border control agents and outfitting them with better equipment and more advanced technology to calling up the U.S. military to patrol the border with Mexico.

Contending that drastically reducing immigration from Mexico would have dire consequences for the American economy, immigration advocates oppose most of these measures. Instead, many support President George W. Bush's plan for a guest worker program with Mexico, which would match foreign workers with American employers when no Americans can be found to fill the jobs. In Bush's program, illegal immigrants already in the country and foreign nationals wishing to enter could register with the government to work in the United States for three years; they would later have the option of signing up for an additional three years. These temporary workers would be given legal status, but they would be sent home after completing the program.

One of the main benefits of Bush's guest worker plan, supporters argue, is that it would protect America's national security. As President Bush asserted when he introduced the program in January 2004:

> Our homeland will be more secure when we can better account for those who enter our country, instead of the current situation in which millions of people are ... unknown

to the law. Law enforcement will face fewer problems with undocumented workers and will be better able to focus on the true threats to our nation from criminals and terrorists. And when temporary workers can travel legally and freely, there will be more efficient management of our borders and more effective enforcement against those who pose a danger to our country.

Debate over the proposed temporary-worker plan continues. Supporters contend that it is a practical solution to a significant problem and benefits both employers and illegal aliens. Critics of the plan view it as a veiled attempt to legitimize illegal immigration and as a step toward complete amnesty for illegal aliens. Tom Tancredo, a Republican congressman from Colorado, has criticized Bush for stating that his program would bring illegal workers "out of the shadows." "Bringing workers out of the shadows is simply another way of saying we should legalize illegal immigrants," Tancredo said. "Yes, we should bring illegal immigrants out of the shadows, and then return them to their home country." The debate over the guest worker program as well as other border policies is covered in this chapter.

> "A nation penetrated every year by some 300,000 illegal aliens . . . is not a nation experiencing 'immigration.' It is a nation experiencing invasion and conquest."

America Should Militarize Its Borders

Sam Francis

In the following viewpoint Sam Francis maintains that the influx of illegal aliens across America's southern border is tantamount to an invasion. Because the federal government is obligated to protect the states from foreign invasion, Francis contends, it should place American troops along the border to stop illegal immigration. As a syndicated columnist, Francis wrote on such topics as immigration, gun rights, right-wing politics, and multiculturalism. He died on February 15, 2005.

As you read, consider the following questions:

1. How many legal and illegal aliens settle in the United States each year, according to statistics cited by Francis?
2. On what grounds does the author oppose granting amnesty to illegal immigrants living in the United States?
3. According to Francis, what are the political implications of granting amnesty?

A tip of the hat to Sen. Trent Lott of Mississippi, the once and future Senate Majority Leader, who ... endorsed putting U.S. soldiers on the border with Mexico to protect the country against illegal immigrant invasion.

Mr. Lott is the highest ranking public office holder yet to support that position, and precisely because he is, others may follow.

This is what leadership means.

The senator's remarks were made in an interview with Fox News' Bill O'Reilly, on Nov. 7 [2002].

"Why not back up the Border Patrol with military, whether it's National Guard or straight troops—why not do it?" Mr. O'Reilly asked.

"Well, I think we should do it," the senator replied.

"Do you really? ... You're the first politician I've heard [say so]," Mr. O'Reilly said.

"Well, look," the senator explained. "Most politicians run around worried about civil libertarians and being sued by the ACLU [American Civil Liberties Union]. This is not only a porous border in terms of illegal aliens. It's also a porous border in terms of crime and drugs."

The senator is entirely correct about that, of course, and there's every good reason to send in the troops for those reasons alone.

Invasion and Conquest

But the fact is that a nation penetrated every year by some 300,000 illegal aliens and in which some 11 million illegal aliens live permanently is not a nation experiencing "immigration." It is a nation experiencing invasion and conquest—and that's not counting the legal immigrants.

"More than 1.2 million legal and illegal immigrants combined now settle in the United States each year," the Center for Immigration Studies reported in January, 2001. "The number of immigrants living in the United States has more than

Militarize the Borders

A few thousand border agents here or there are not going to stop the hordes of mysterious characters streaming across our borders and the violent drug and human smuggling cartels trafficking in our cities. The imperative to immediately deploy our National Guard, Air Guard, Army Reserves and even our regular army to our southern and northern borders and ports could not be greater than what it is today.

Many oppose the militarization of our borders for fear of offending Mexico and Canada. Which is better; a realistic respectful accountable relationship with our neighboring countries or bombs going off in our subways and shopping malls?

Chuck Busch, "Senatorial Surrender at the Border," OpinionEditorials.com, July 24, 2005.

tripled since 1970. . . . By historical standards, the number of immigrants living in the United States is unprecedented. Even at the peak of the great wave of early 20th century immigration, the number of immigrants living in the United States was less than half what it is today."

The legal invasion is our own fault—because our own laws and lawmakers allow the aliens to come and stay—but the illegal invasion that Sen. Lott is talking about is only partly our fault, which is what the senator wishes to correct.

Drugs, criminals and even illegal aliens really are law enforcement problems that should not ordinarily be handled by the military. Invasion is another matter entirely—not simply one of law enforcement but of national security. The federal government under the Constitution has the obligation to protect the states against invasion, and the military is the only public agency capable of carrying out that duty. President Bush says he's opposed to putting troops on the border, though he at least seems to have placed his idiotic idea of amnesty for illegal aliens on the shelf for a while. Prior to Sept. 11, 2001, he and the administration were pushing amnesty, and Mexico's President Vicente Fox is still hot for it, since it would legalize millions of his own citizens inside this country and swell Mexican political power within our own borders immensely.

Pressure for Amnesty

Even before Mr. Lott called for protecting the border with troops, President Fox was threatening to mobilize his Mexican millions to pressure the U.S. government for amnesty.

"Disappointed by the lack of progress towards a migration accord," the London *Financial Times* reported ... ("migration accord" is the currently favored euphemism for amnesty),

> Mexico is preparing to launch its own campaign to convince U.S. legislators and the public of the benefits of legalizing millions of Mexican workers.
>
> Mexico's government ... will probably begin its efforts ... in key states with large Latino populations: California, Texas, Florida, Illinois and New York. There are 35 million Latinos in the U.S., some two-thirds of whom are of Mexican descent. It is hoping to repeat its success in swaying public opinion in favor of the North American Free Trade Agreement (NAFTA), which took effect in 1994 and has led to an explosion of trade between the countries.

Even without amnesty, then, Mexico is already a major player in American politics, precisely because of its huge population inside our borders. Legalizing the remaining millions who are here illegally would only multiply its power and encourage millions of others to come, legally or not.

Amnesty and protecting our borders are two different issues, but they're not unrelated. By putting troops on the border, the president would not only halt the invasion but also tell the Mexican government that encourages it to stay within its own borders and mind its own business.

With President Fox brazenly threatening to use his own population as a political blackjack to force his wishes on this country, it's well past time for our government to tell him so.

"Having the military enforce the immigration laws isn't wise, it isn't necessary, and it's not legal."

America Should Not Militarize Its Borders

Gene Healy

Gene Healy is a senior editor at the Cato Institute, a libertarian public policy organization. He writes on such topics as federalism, constitutional war powers, and criminal justice. In the following viewpoint he argues that administration officials are right to resist the calls from some politicians and political pundits to deploy American troops to the U.S.-Mexican border to stem the flow of illegal immigration. He asserts that it is illegal and dangerous to use soldiers to do law enforcement duty.

As you read, consider the following questions:

1. According to the author, why is it dangerous for the U.S. military to protect the U.S.-Mexico border?
2. Why do Pentagon officials oppose placing troops on the borders, as reported by Healy?
3. What restrictions does the Posse Comitatus Act place on troops, according to the author?

The U.S. military is the most effective fighting force in history—so effective, in fact, that politicians and pundits have come to see it as a panacea for every security problem posed by the terrorist threat. But on the home front there are many tasks for which the military is ill-suited and where its deployment would be ineffective and dangerous.

Nowhere is that clearer than with the growing calls to militarize our borders. Politicians like Rep. Tom Tancredo (R.-Colo.) and Sen. Trent Lott (R.-Miss.) and conservative pundits like Bill O'Reilly and Michelle Malkin want armed soldiers to enforce U.S. immigration law. In her new bestseller *Invasion: How America Still Welcomes Terrorists, Criminals, and Other Foreign Menaces to Our Shores,* Malkin writes that "at the northern border with Canada . . . every rubber orange cone and measly 'No Entry' sign should immediately be replaced with an armed National Guardsman." She suggests that something in the neighborhood of 100,000 troops might be appropriate.

The problem with this idea is that the same training that makes U.S. soldiers outstanding warriors makes them extremely dangerous as cops. Lawrence Korb, former assistant secretary of defense in the Reagan administration, put it succinctly: The military "is trained to vaporize, not Mirandize."

No one knows this better than the military establishment, which is why the Pentagon has consistently resisted calls to station troops on our borders, most recently in the spring of last year [2002], when Congress pushed for border militarization. Pentagon officials raised the possibility of an "unlawful and potentially lethal use of force incident" if the troops were armed. Ultimately, some 1,600 National Guardsmen were placed at the Mexican and Canadian borders for a six-month mission, most of them unarmed. A Pentagon official told United Press International, "We don't like to do these things. We do them as a matter of last resort. That's why we entered into this undertaking with a specific end date and a specific requirement."

The Hernandez Tragedy

The Pentagon was right to worry. U.S. troops have been placed on the borders in the past, as part of the quixotic fight against drug smuggling. Even though those deployments have been limited to surveillance and support roles, they've led to tragedy. In 1997, a Marine anti-drug patrol shot and killed 18-year-old high school student Esquiel Hernandez, who was carrying a .22 caliber rifle while tending goats on his own farm in Redford, Texas near the Mexican border. The Justice Department paid out $1.9 million to the Hernandez family as settlement of a wrongful death lawsuit.

The Hernandez incident should be a cautionary tale for those who seek to militarize our borders. An internal Pentagon investigation of the incident noted that the soldiers were ill-prepared for contact with civilians, as their military training instilled "an aggressive spirit while teaching basic combat skills."

Because of the restrictions imposed by the Posse Comitatus Act, the federal law that proscribes the military from "executing the laws," the Marines who killed Hernandez operated under rules of engagement that prevented them from arresting or otherwise directly engaging civilians. Nonetheless, according to a senior FBI agent involved with the case, "The Marines perceived a target-practicing shot as a threat to their safety. . . . From that point, their training and instincts took over to neutralize a threat." The camouflaged Marines tailed Hernandez for 20 minutes, and failed to identify themselves or try to defuse the situation. When Hernandez raised his rifle again, a Marine shot him, and let him bleed to death without attempting to administer first aid.

The new proposals to use troops for border patrol work would greatly multiply the dangers revealed by the Hernandez incident. Unlike the soldiers deployed for the drug war, the troops on border patrol duty would be given arrest authority and allowed to directly engage civilians. The danger to civilians wouldn't be limited to border areas either, given that fed-

Enforce Existing Laws

Many experts agree the way to lessen illegal border crossings is not to militarize the border, but to enforce immigration laws already in place. For instance, it is against the law to hire illegal immigrants, but last year [2003] only 13 employers were fined for doing so. That kind of lax enforcement does nothing to discourage employers—or illegal immigrants who know they won't be turned away, says Mark Krikorian, executive director of the Center for Immigration Studies in Washington.

"We need to reduce the magnet that pulls the illegal aliens as well as doing a better job holding the line," he says.

Kris Axtman and Peter Grier,
Christian Science Monitor, *December 10, 2004.*

eral law allows the Border Patrol to set up checkpoints as far as 100 miles inland from the border or shoreline.

Having the military enforce the immigration laws isn't wise, it isn't necessary, and it's not legal. Both the INS [Immigration and Naturalization Service] and the Border Patrol are getting a half a billion dollar infusion of new resources, and rapidly hiring new agents. If still more border patrol personnel are needed, they should be hired. But border security can be provided without eroding America's tradition of civil-military separation.

> "The central idea is to ... give most of
> the people who would otherwise come
> illegally a safe, orderly, legal option."

America Should Develop a Guest Worker Program

Tamar Jacoby

The following viewpoint is excerpted from a speech by Tamar Jacoby, a senior fellow at the Manhattan Institute, a conservative public policy research organization. She advocates creating a guest worker program that would allow Mexican workers to enter the United States legally to work. Such a program, she contends, is the most realistic way to manage the flow of immigrant workers, meet the labor needs of U.S. businesses, protect national security, and restore the rule of law in America.

As you read, consider the following questions:

1. What are the author's four criteria for a viable immigration policy?
2. In what ways does illegal immigration undermine the rule of law, in Jacoby's opinion?
3. How can the American government eliminate the black market for cheap labor, according to the author?

Not only on the border, but also in the workplace, enforcement of our immigration law is close to meaningless. In

Tamar Jacoby, "Immigration Reform: Politics and Prospects," *The American Enterprise*, January 10, 2005. Copyright © 2005 by *The American Enterprise*, a national magazine of Politics, Business, and Culture. www.TAEmag.com. Reproduced by permission.

many places in America, immigrants have overwhelmed the social services—to the point that schools and emergency rooms don't work for native-born Americans. Personally, I'm optimistic about assimilation—and we can talk more about that later if you like. But it's far from certain that today's immigrants will assimilate successfully, and if they don't—if the dire scenarios are even close to right—it will spell disaster for the nation's future. So it's not enough to claim or even prove that immigrants are good for the economy. "We're not just an economy, we're a nation," as Patrick Buchanan likes to say. And we still have to manage the flow in a way that works for us as a nation.

And that's not as easy as it sounds. I think we've seen why closing the border is no option. But neither is just opening the gates a possibility. We can't let every poor, hungry Mexican or poor, hungry Chinese come and try their luck in America. So we're back to where we started. We need to find a middle course. But what exactly is that middle course? What is the immigration policy that makes sense in today's increasingly integrated but dangerous world?

Well, I submit to you, the compromise has to meet four criteria. I think they're all obvious—painfully obvious. But astonishingly, our current immigration policy doesn't meet a single one of them.

Hardheaded and Realistic

First, without question, the compromise has to be in our interest—our national interest. Immigration policy isn't a suicide pact. Nice as it is to be altruistic or to be a good neighbor, I don't think we owe would-be immigrants anything. This, in my view, is where much of the pro-immigrant camp gets it wrong, and even President Bush, I believe, is on the wrong track when he talks about "compassion" with regard to immigration policy. Immigration policy has to be hardheaded, and it has to be driven by our needs as a nation.

Second, also pretty obvious, I think, but hardly true today, our immigration policy ought to be realistic. We ought to start by acknowledging the reality of the global marketplace. We ought to accept that we can't or aren't going to turn off the flow. (And this of course is where the restrictionist camp is most seriously wrong—they pretend we can just turn off the faucet.) And we also ought to accept the reality of the existing underground economy, which some economists estimate may account for as much as 10 percent of American business today. Sound policy would acknowledge both of these realities—the flow and the underground pool it has created—and bring them above ground. I'm switching metaphors—and forgive me—but let's get serious and acknowledge this tiger and figure out how to ride it, rather than letting it ride us.

Third, also so obvious that it hardly needs arguing, we've got to do a better job of securing our borders. As is, several hundreds of thousands of unauthorized people walk across the border into our country every year—without benefit of background checks or controls of any kind. And in an age of global terrorism, obviously, that's unacceptable. But—and here's where I part company from the restrictionists—since we're not going to stop this traffic, we've got to create a way for most of the people to come legally so we can zero in on the tiny handful who pose a real threat.

Restoring the Rule of Law

Fourth and finally, there can be no question: not only must we regain control of our borders, but—arguably even more important—we must restore the rule of law in our communities. Here too, the restrictionists are right—or at least half right. "What part of 'illegal' don't you understand?" they ask. And it is a question that bothers many Americans—and understandably so. Of all the costs that come with illegal immigration, none is more corrosive than its consequences for the rule of law.

It's not just the vast underground communities where most people shrug at the law on a daily basis. It's not just the entire American industries that operate on the wrong side of the rules, relying on international criminal cartels to recruit the workers they need to keep their businesses open. It's not just the millions—literally millions—of fake names and the sea of false documents that go with them. And it's not just the taxes we're forfeiting, which Barron's . . . estimated may run into the hundreds of billions of dollars. We [are] sacrificing something much more important and more valuable than all of this—and that's our essential character as a law-abiding nation. Both our prosperity and our freedoms are based on that rule of law—I'm sure I don't have to explain that to anyone in this room—and we're putting it at risk.

Another way to think about this: consider what we're asking the American people to swallow. It's one thing—and quite a request, by the way—to ask them to accept a million, maybe a million and a half, new immigrants in their midst every year. A million and a half non-English-speaking foreigners, many of them uneducated and unskilled, who may or may not ultimately fit in here. But as things stand now, we're also asking the American people to accept an inevitable end to the rule of law as they know it—guaranteed, routine, ongoing illegality in their neighborhoods and workplaces. It's an unthinkable request—no matter how good immigrants are for our economy. But that's exactly what we're asking—that's what's happening. And we've got to do something about it—something dramatic.

Bush's Plan

So those are my four criteria. And where do they leave us? What's the immigration policy that makes sense for the United States today? Well, I hope it doesn't come as an anticlimax, but I believe that President Bush was very much on the right

Enhancing Security

America is advocating human rights all over the world but what about the ten million here at home who are constantly living under the fear of deportation?. . .

A just legalization program will allow hard-working, law-abiding individuals to come out of the shadows to be screened by the government. It will also make the communities safer because, when immigrants' deportation fears are removed, they are more likely to report crimes and suspicious activity to local law enforcement agencies. This measure enhances security by bringing immigration under the rule of law, enabling law enforcement agencies to focus on terrorists and criminals rather than workers and families.

Ranjit Shaji, "Justice, Freedom, and Liberty
for Undocumented People," OpinionEditorials.com,
July 20, 2005.

track with the principles he announced almost exactly a year ago [in 2004]. He didn't get everything right—and I think he knew it. That's why he announced only principles. He didn't say, "Read my lips." He said this is a first draft, and he challenged Congress to go to work filling in the details. But as first drafts go, I think his was pretty good. I think it meets all four of the criteria I just laid out, and I think it stands a good chance of restoring the integrity of our broken system.

I'm sure you know the outlines of his plan. The central idea is to connect willing workers with willing employees—not to create a new flow or add to the total number that enter the county each year, but merely to give most of the people who would otherwise come illegally a safe, orderly, legal option. The president proposes to do that with a guest worker program—a program, first and foremost, for those on the other side of the border and contemplating the trip.

Second, you can't build a legal structure on an illegal foundation—and you can't expect most employers to use a guest worker program if they still have access to millions of unauthorized laborers already here in the United States. So in addition to enlarging the pipeline into the country, we also need to eliminate the existing black market. This is no easy task: we're talking, after all, about eight to 12 million people, maybe more. But the president proposes to get rid of it by creating a path to legalization—by asking illegal workers who can otherwise prove their bona fides to come forward and pay a penalty and get on the right side of the law, and then we would allow them to participate in the guest worker program.

This is, of course, the most controversial part of the proposal—and, I believe, the most misunderstood. The Bush plan isn't an amnesty. The president isn't suggesting we just wave a wand and tell people that what they did wrong doesn't matter. What he's offering them is a chance to earn their way in out of the shadows—not only for their sake, but for ours. Because short of deporting them—short of arresting and removing eight to 12 million people—that's the only way we're going to eliminate the existing black market and create a solid foundation on which to build a new, legal system.

So those are the two key components—a provision for those coming and one for those already here. And going back to our criteria, what stands out for me is the president's realism. He recognizes that the all-important first step in addressing the problem is accepting the reality of international supply and demand. He understands the business need for a steady stream of reliable workers. And he grasps that the goal of policy should be to manage and make the most of the market-driven flow, not try futilely to interdict it. And this is nothing short of revolutionary—commonsensical, maybe, but still, in the circumstances, revolutionary.

> *"For our country's good—and for the good of agriculture itself—we need to reject calls for a new guest-worker program and to get serious about enforcing existing immigration law."*

America Should Not Develop a Guest Worker Program

Mark Krikorian

In the following viewpoint Mark Krikorian argues against the creation of a guest worker program with Mexico. He maintains that such a program would have a negative impact on the American economy, particularly the agricultural sector. Allowing farmers to depend on cheap imported labor, he insists, keeps wages low and prevents innovation that would lead to more efficient farming methods. Krikorian is executive director of the Center for Immigration Studies and a visiting fellow at the Nixon Center. He has written extensively on the subject of immigration policy.

As you read, consider the following questions:

1. How many Mexican farmworkers are allowed to enter the United States legally through H2-A visas every year, according to Krikorian?
2. What was the Bracero program, as described by the author?

3. What point does the author make by contrasting the examples of Florida cane growers with California grape growers?

During President Bush's recent visit to Mexico, he and Mexican President Vicente Fox agreed to establish an "orderly framework for migration" between the two countries. Among the proposals that their newly formed immigration working group will review is a temporary work program for Mexicans—many of whom now come to the United States illegally. This would represent an expansion of the current H2-A guest-worker visas, which allow some 30,000 farm workers to enter the country legally each year.

Increasing the number of guest workers is not a new idea. Last year [2000], I testified before the House Judiciary Subcommittee on Immigration and Claims against a bill that would have created a large agricultural guest-worker program for the first time since the so-called Bracero program, which brought close to 5 million Mexican farm workers to the United States between 1942 and 1964. Sens. Phil Gramm (R-Tex.) and Bob Graham (D-Fla.) plan to introduce dueling guest-worker proposals later this year. These have the potential to dwarf the Bracero program, since there are some 3 million Mexican illegals already here, and Gramm's proposal would not be limited to agriculture.

A Misguided Approach

This is a misguided approach. My concern is not solely about the detrimental effects of encouraging more people to cross the border to work in this country—although I do believe that today's mass immigration is causing severe social and economic problems. I'm also concerned about the negative impact the policy will have on American agriculture.

There's a widely held belief that large swaths of our economy could not function without low-skilled, low-wage foreign laborers. In Gramm's words, "They are vital to our economy, yet they are violating our laws." However a careful examination of fruit and vegetable production demonstrates not only that our economy can do perfectly well without foreign labor, but that the large-scale availability of such labor actually impedes economic progress.

Similar claims about the importance of imported farm workers to maintain the superiority of American agriculture have been made in the past. In the early 1960s, during the hearings that led to the termination of the Bracero program because of exploitation of Mexican workers, a spokesman for tomato farmers claimed that "the use of braceros [imported laborers] is absolutely essential to the survival of the tomato industry." Congress went ahead and discontinued the program (which is still mired in controversy, with lawyers representing braceros preparing to file suit to recover money deducted from bracero pay). Without the cheap Mexican labor, farmers increasingly mechanized the harvest over the next three decades, resulting in a quadrupling in the production of tomatoes destined for processing—and a fall in real prices.

The Threat of Guest-Worker Programs

This result nicely summarizes the threat guest-worker programs (or large-scale illegal immigration) pose to America's agricultural competitiveness: By artificially inflating the supply of labor, the government's interference in the labor market keeps wages low, resulting in slowed mechanization, and stagnating productivity in fruit and vegetable production.

The period from 1960 to 1975—roughly from the end of the Bracero program to the beginning of the mass illegal immigration we are experiencing today—was a period of considerable mechanization, with the average labor hours per acre used in harvesting fruits and vegetables dropping by about 20 percent. But a continuing increase in the acreage and number of crops harvested mechanically did not materialize as ex-

What America Has Learned

The U.S. experience with foreign farm workers leads to three major lessons:

- *There is nothing more permanent than temporary workers.* After farm employers and foreign workers become dependent on each other, the farmers do not think about alternatives . . . , and the migrants need U.S. earnings to maintain their families.

- *The availability of foreign workers distorts the economy.* Farmers take into account many factors when they decide whether to plant apples in remote areas of Washington or West Virginia, especially likely revenues and costs in four or five years when there are apples to pick. But they do not have to worry about the availability of pickers if there is a guest worker program. An auto executive might be fired for putting a plant in a remote area without workers; a farmer feels entitled to foreign workers to make the investment profitable.

- *Employers invest in lobbying to maintain the program, not in labor-saving or back-saving alternatives.* Legislation authorizing farmers to hire guest workers has usually been considered a temporary bridge, a way for farmers to get crops harvested until soldiers returned from war or mechanization eliminated the need for hand workers. However, once a guest worker program is in place, farmers invest in lobbying to maintain the program, not in labor-saving and productivity-increasing alternatives.

Philip Martin, Center for Immigration Studies, April 2000.

pected after 1975, in large part because the supply of workers was artificially swollen by the growth in illegal immigration.

Farmers' mass access to foreign workers (illegal or legal) has caused the wages of farm workers to decrease over the past decade. A March 2000 report from the Labor Department found that the real wages of farm workers fell from $6.89 per hour in 1989 to $6.18 per hour in 1998. A new guest-worker program, or continued official acquiescence to illegal immigration, is likely to continue this downward trend. This may seem superficially appealing to farmers, but from a competitive point of view, vying with low-wage countries on the basis of labor costs is a dead end. No modern society will ever be willing to reduce farm workers' wages enough to match those paid in Third World countries.

Hampering Modernization

You can see how changing the labor market plays out in the fields. Through the 1980s, sugar companies in Florida imported West Indian guest workers to harvest cane by hand. Then the industry was hit by a wave of lawsuits filed on behalf of workers whose contracts had been violated. This proved so nettlesome that the growers calculated it would be more profitable to mechanize the sugar harvest than to honor farm worker contracts. Today, virtually all Florida sugar cane is harvested by machine, resulting in dramatic increases in productivity, higher wages and more civilized working conditions for the remaining workers. In short, cutting off the stream of foreign labor promoted dramatic steps toward modernization.

The raisin crop provides a graphic example of the opposite phenomenon. Raisin grapes, grown in California's Central Valley, are the most labor-intensive commercial crop in North America. Traditionally, the grapes are cut with a knife, placed in a pan, then laid on a paper tray for drying. During the drying period, they must be manually turned, then rolled and collected. But a new cultivation method, called "dried-on-the-vine" (DOV) production, promises both radical reductions in labor demand and improvements in quality. This innovative method has not been widely adopted in the United States precisely because the widespread availability of foreign workers is a disincentive to raisin farmers to make the long-term capital investment needed to retrofit existing raisin farms for DOV production.

Lagging Behind

There is also the danger that the slowed innovation caused by artificial infusions of labor will allow other developed countries to leap ahead of us. This is probably most striking in the cutting-edge field of robotic harvesting. Though still in its infancy, great progress has been made in this third wave of agricultural mechanization. But because of the mass availability of alien labor in the United States, the European Union is well ahead of us in using the potentially revolutionary technology. Enactment of a new guest-worker program may help our competitors gain a permanent advantage over us in agriculture—an area where America has traditionally been the pacesetter.

It's heartening to see Bush and Fox engage on some of the major issues that confront our two countries. But, whatever final form their new framework for migration takes, the American president would do well to resist the siren song of legalized foreign labor. It may look attractive in the short term, but in the long term, it threatens to undermine the commercial viability of American agriculture. For our country's good—and for the good of agriculture itself—we need to reject calls for a new guest-worker program and to get serious about enforcing existing immigration law.

> "The aim of the Minutemen all along has been to highlight the issue of illegal immigration, and, if all the media attention is any indication, they have succeeded."

Civilian Patrols Should Be Encouraged on the Border

Cinnamon Stillwell

In 2005 a group of citizen volunteers called the Minutemen patrolled a twenty-three-mile stretch of the Arizona-Mexico border and reported sightings of illegal immigrants to Border Patrol officials. In the following viewpoint Cinnamon Stillwell praises the actions of the Minutemen and similar groups. She contends that such efforts have brought much-needed publicity to the problem of illegal immigration and the government's failure to address the issue. Stillwell is a columnist for SFGate.com and Frontpagemag.com. Her columns also appear at IntellectualConservative.com and IsraelNationalNews.com and in the Jewish Press.

As you read, consider the following questions:

1. How have the Minutemen been portrayed by the mainstream press, according to Stillwell?
2. According to the author, how have pro-immigration activists skewed the immigration debate?

3. How have the Minutemen's efforts benefited Border Patrol agents in Arizona, as reported by the author?

It isn't just the weather that's heating up this month [April 2005] along the Arizona-Mexico border. Fed up with a largely unresponsive government, an understaffed Border Patrol and the daily flood of illegal immigrants into the United States, civilian patrols have volunteered to guard a 23-mile stretch of the border in southeast Arizona. They are members of the Minuteman Project, a grassroots effort designed to call attention to what has become a virtual invasion from south of the border.

As a testament to the volatility surrounding the issue of illegal immigration, the Minutemen (and Minutewomen) are causing a national uproar. Despite the fact that members are simply reporting illegal sightings to the Border Patrol, much like any Neighborhood Watch system throughout the country, opponents have portrayed them as trigger-happy rednecks out for blood. They have been largely vilified by the mainstream media and even by President Bush, who accused them of being "vigilantes."

In fact, the Minutemen include Americans from all races and walks of life with one belief in common—that the immigration fiasco cannot continue unabated. Poll after poll shows that a majority of the country agrees with the Minutemen—in philosophy if not in tactics—and many must be wondering why protecting America's national sovereignty is even an issue. As U.S. Rep. Tom Tancredo of Colorado put it during a Minuteman rally . . . , "You are good citizens who ask only that our laws be enforced. When did that become a radical idea?"

Rendering Citizenship Meaningless

The open-borders lobby has been so effective in skewing the discussion of immigration that some Americans have indeed convinced themselves that enforcing immigration laws is not only wrong but also impossible. By steadily increasing the rights of illegal immigrants throughout America and particularly in the Southwest, these activists have succeeded in their efforts to render American citizenship virtually meaningless.

It began with sanctuary cities, where law enforcement personnel are not allowed to question or report criminals' immigration status. Then it was all about giving illegal immigrants in-state tuition at colleges and universities (which reeks of discrimination against out-of-state American students who are not afforded such privileges) and free health care and bank accounts, and it continues today with the ongoing crusade to grant driver's licenses to illegal immigrants. The right to vote in public school elections is being pushed now, and it's just a matter of time before voting in political elections gets added to the mix.

One of the more popular arguments the open-borders lobby makes is that illegal immigrants simply do "the jobs Americans don't want." This insulting claim ignores that there was a time when Americans cared for their own children, cleaned their own toilets, painted and built their own houses and did their own gardening. Many still do, as a matter of fact. But now Americans are told that they're "above" such work and must rely on an immigrant underclass to do it for them. Sounds a bit like Saudi Arabia. Somehow, I doubt that's a society most Americans want to emulate.

Others argue that America profits from the cheap labor illegal immigration affords, but the truth is that the expense to taxpayers far outweighs the benefits. All across the country, and particularly here in California, state budgets are going bust, hospitals are closing down, public schools are unable to cope with the influx of foreign language speakers, social services are overwhelmed and local law enforcement is being cut. It turns out that illegal immigration does come with a price tag our nation can ill afford.

The Efforts of Immigration Activists

Immigration activists have altered the very language of the issue so that illegal immigrants are referred to as undocumented workers and day laborers. All immigration is lumped together, whether illegal or otherwise, to blur the lines between the two categories. This blending allows all opponents of illegal immigration to be labeled "anti-immigrant." Such activists are particularly fond of using the term *racist* to silence anyone who dares to question the open-borders orthodoxy.

The myth that opposition to illegal immigration in America comes solely from white people continues to be perpetuated, but the reality defies the stereotype. Americans of all backgrounds, and particularly Hispanics whose families have lived in the United States for generations as well as legal immigrants from Latin countries and elsewhere, count themselves among the growing forces of those opposed to illegal immigration. The late revered Latino labor activist Cesar Chavez was in fact a firm opponent of illegal immigration; he understood that it would undermine wages for American farm workers. Was Chavez also a racist? What's truly racist is the perpetuation of a subculture of unintegrated Hispanic laborers in America.

The open-borders lobby is certainly a big tent and shares as its constituency many seemingly disparate groups. Democrats catering to their liberal base, including the ACLU [American Civil Liberties Union] and other groups devoted to the "civil rights" of illegal immigrants, figure prominently. Then there are Hispanic advocacy groups such as the National Council of La Raza (the Race), MALDEF (the Mexican American Legal Defense and Educational Fund) and MECHa (Movimiento Estudiantil Chicano de Aztlan), which openly calls for the "liberation" of "occupied Aztlan" (the American Southwest). Business interests intent on retaining dirt-cheap labor are also part of the problem. Furthermore, both the Republican and Democratic parties pander to the Hispanic vote, despite the fact that it's often quite conservative toward immigration and a host of other issues.

Bush's Policies Puzzling

As for George W. Bush, he has little in common with his fellow Republicans when it comes to illegal immigration. Although more than a few Republican politicians and business leaders support his policies, he's in danger of losing touch with his base on this issue. Many people are puzzled as to why Bush signed the U.S. Terrorism Reform and Prevention Act in 2004, which called for 2,000 more Border Patrol agents per year, and then proposed only enough funding in 2006 for a measly 210.

But it's Bush's guest worker proposal that has Republicans up in arms. The plan is somewhat reminiscent of the World War II–inspired bracero program, which didn't exactly leave a successful legacy. But many observers feel that the proposal is really just an amnesty plan by another name and as such simply recycles past failures. Earlier amnesty plans resulted only in further illegal immigration, and, judging by the influx immediately following Bush's announcement, little has changed. One wonders whether the oft-touted "genius" of Karl Rove, the president's chief political strategist, isn't a tad overrated when seen in this light.

Mexico's Response to the Minutemen

Though illegal immigration encompasses all nationalities, by far the largest chunk comes from Mexico, and, for many open-borders opponents, Bush's cozy relationship with Mexican President Vicente Fox is at the heart of the matter. Fox is best known for constantly whining that America isn't doing enough to subsidize his country's citizenry, while he simultaneously offers nothing in return. He was an active opponent of the war in Iraq and refused to commit Mexican troops. Meanwhile, he acts as if Mexico is doing America a favor by selling

The Minuteman Project Is Successful

The controversy surrounding the Minuteman Project is a poorly crafted red herring.

The simple, empirical reality is the Minuteman Project has been hugely successful. Illegal border crossings along the stretch of Arizona/Mexico border have virtually been stopped.

Notwithstanding the fears of vigilante violence and gap-toothed, redneck pick up truck marauders, the Minuteman Project is a well organized and effectively managed deterrent to a chronic travesty of neglect.

Geoff Metcalf, NewsMax.com, April 11, 2005.

us its oil. Fox's latest demand has been for the United States to tear down the fence between San Diego and Tijuana, presumably to make it even easier for illegal immigrants to cross the border.

Fox's reaction to the Minuteman Project has been predictably indignant. Along with increasing troop strength along the border, he had the gall to threaten to take the group to court. Latin American gangs, who take full advantage of the open border to trade in guns, drugs and humans, have gone so far as to threaten the lives of the Minutemen. And, according to the Border Patrol, the Mexican military is now actively helping illegal immigrants, including known drug runners, reach safer border-crossing points in order to avoid the Minutemen. No doubt this little citizen uprising didn't figure into the handbook on how to enter the U.S. illegally the Mexican government distributed to citizens last year [2004].

Of course, it's in the interest of Fox and the rest of Mexico's ruling elite to further the current situation. Remittances, or funds sent home from immigrants, to Mexicans now surpass revenue from both foreign investors and tourism. And as long as Mexicans have the escape valve of America, they are less likely to advocate for much-needed reform at home. Whatever the underpinnings, Fox's arrogance and Bush's slavish devotion are becoming increasingly nauseating to a fed-up American populace. The Minutemen may have put it best when they accused Bush of being the "co-president of Mexico."

After the terrorist attacks of 9/11, one would think that border security might be a top priority for the United States, but the truth is that illegal immigration has actually increased since then.

Leadership from Congress

Due to the appalling lack of leadership on the matter, many Republicans feel left out in the cold. However, they may have found a politician who represents their interests in Republican Congressman Tom Tancredo, a leading voice in the effort to battle illegal immigration. Another front-runner is U.S. Rep. James Sensenbrenner of Wisconsin, sponsor of the federal Real ID Act, which would effectively end the quest to grant driver's licenses to illegal immigrants. Although the bill has its opponents on both sides of the political fence, the growing alarm of the open-borders lobby is a testament to its potential effectiveness.

As for Democrats, if they really want to usurp the Republicans in the next election, they should do so from the Right and tackle illegal immigration. Sen. Hillary Clinton may already have figured that one out, judging by her statements . . . on the subject. Even a few conservatives have hinted that they'd vote for the wildly-unpopular-on-the-right Hillary if she delivered the goods, although most are too suspicious of her motives. One thing's for sure: The question of illegal immigration is likely to loom over the next presidential election.

Taking Up the Torch

In the meantime, it's the Minutemen who are taking up the torch of immigration reform, and it looks like they may have made some progress. Although the Department of Homeland Security claims there's no relation, it's hardly a coincidence that Arizona is suddenly getting 500 new Border Patrol agents and 23 aircraft to patrol the border, and that 155 officers are on the way. And, in what may be a good sign, a group of Republican lawmakers recently made the trek to Tombstone, Ariz., to show their support for the Minutemen.

But the group is also taking heat for its activism. Volunteers from the ACLU in Arizona have been subjecting the Minutemen to daily surveillance, even going so far as to alert coyotes (human smugglers) and illegal immigrants that they're in the vicinity. And, although they've been trying desperately to catch the Minutemen in some wrongdoing, their efforts so far have been futile. Recent accusations that the Minutemen "detained" an illegal alien, who they in fact gave food and water, turned out to be unsubstantiated. The Minutemen have also run into some resistance from local authorities in Cochise County; the county zoning commission is reportedly unfairly targeting the Miracle Valley Bible College, which houses Minuteman volunteers.

Despite the obstacles, the aim of the Minutemen all along has been to highlight the issue of illegal immigration, and, if all the media attention is any indication, they have succeeded. Demonstrating the Minutemen's growing influence further, other citizen groups are now considering following suit. As project organizer and Vietnam veteran Jim Gilchrist put it, "We have already accomplished our goal a hundredfold . . . we've got our message out to the American public." Whether Bush and America's leadership are listening remains to be seen.

"Amid the copper-colored mountains and lush-but-thorny desert of Southeast Arizona, the vigilante legacy of the Earp boys has never completely died away."

Civilian Patrols Endanger Illegal Immigrants

Bob Moser

In the following viewpoint Bob Moser reports on the efforts of vigilante groups patrolling the U.S.-Mexico border in Arizona. He contends that the extreme anti-immigrant rhetoric and aggressive tactics used by these groups endanger the lives of illegal immigrants attempting to cross the border. Moser is a former John S. Knight Fellow at Stanford University. His articles on immigration, politics, and social issues have appeared in the Nation, Rolling Stone, *and the* Independent Weekly.

As you read, consider the following questions:

1. Why has southern Arizona become the most popular place to illegally cross the U.S.-Mexico border in recent years, as reported by the author?

2. What message did the actions of the Hanigan family send to would-be migrants, according to Moser?

3. What will end the vigilantism in Arizona, according to Dusty Escapule, as quoted by the author?

In 1881, it took just 30 seconds and 25 gunshots at the O.K. Corral to stamp this tiny border town [Tombstone, Arizona] onto the national imagination. This past October [2002], it took just one editorial in an error-prone local newspaper to turn this Old West tourist trap—and the mean, green border country in which it sits—into a symbol of how vehement and reckless America's anti-immigration movement has become.

"ENOUGH IS ENOUGH!" hollered the banner headline of the Oct. 24 [2002] *Tombstone Tumbleweed*. "A PUBLIC CALL TO ARMS! CITIZENS BORDER PATROL MILITIA NOW FORMING!" In slightly smaller type, *Tumbleweed* owner, publisher and managing editor Chris Simcox exhorted his fellow Arizonans, "JOIN TOGETHER TO PROTECT YOUR COUNTRY IN A TIME OF WAR!"

Simcox was not talking about a war in Iraq. He was talking about a war being fought in the *Tumbleweed*'s back yard, on the border between Mexico and the United States. There, Simcox wrote in language echoing Patrick Buchanan and other anti-immigration extremists, "a swarm of uncontrolled refugees" is "fleeing a marxist structured government" in what amounts to an "invasion" of the U.S. To repel this supposed invasion, Simcox called for drastic measures: a "committee of vigilantes" that would prowl the borderlands, catching immigrants and sending them back south.

The beauty of vigilantism, Simcox wrote, is simple: "We actually have more freedom to tackle the problem than the Government and law enforcement agencies that are bogged down in the quagmire of laws and restrictions."

Anyplace else, the notion that gun-toting private citizens don't have to answer to "laws and restrictions" might sound flat-out ridiculous. But amid the copper-colored mountains and lush-but-thorny desert of Southeast Arizona, the vigilante legacy of the Earp boys has never completely died away. It appeals to folks like Simcox, a transplant from Los Angeles. "The guy is a lunatic," says Tombstone mayor Dusty Escapule, "and is going to get somebody killed."

"I'd Shoot Every Single One"

Simcox is far from alone. Over the last five years, the Wild West mentality has been revived in this desert. With a vengeance.

In the mid-'90s, a major change in U.S. border policy shifted migrants away from urban areas in California and Texas—where access has traditionally been easy—and forced most of them to cross through far harsher terrain. The idea was that crossing through deserts, and over rivers, would deter migrants from making the trip.

Instead, the main result of the policy was to transform southern Arizona into the most popular place to cross from Mexico, with hundreds of thousands making their way through this treacherous desert every year.

Understandably enough, such a state of affairs did not please ranch owners in this combustible corner of Arizona. They found their livestock being stolen or killed for food, their cattle fences being cut, and trash and human waste dotting their land. Several ranchers responded by arming themselves with Colt .45s, M-16s and high-tech surveillance systems to detect "intruders."

At least 20 private citizens have reportedly used their arsenals to apprehend—and, in some cases, abuse and shoot—migrants coming over the border.

"If I had my way," one rancher reportedly bellowed at a meeting with U.S. Border Patrol officials last summer [2002], "I'd shoot every single one of 'em."

Like Open Season

It hasn't quite come to that. But this past fall [2002] the ranchers' "self-defense" efforts—and their fury—not only inspired Simcox, who says he got fed up with the "criminal" immigrants he encountered in Los Angeles; it's also attracted one of the nation's leading anti-immigration extremists, who is using the craziness here to stimulate fear and loathing of immigration across the U.S. And in October [2002], a heavily armed paramilitary group established a "semi-permanent" presence in the area after conducting a two-week hunt for drugs and migrants.

So far, local law enforcers have declined to prosecute apparent acts of vigilantism, though the U.S. Commission on Civil Rights has joined the ACLU [American Civil Liberties Union], the Mexican government, human-rights groups and local governments in calling for an end to the violence. "If you don't prosecute these people for beating Mexican nationals or killing them," says Mayor Escapule, "then it's kind of like open season."

Which is exactly what human-rights advocates fear, as millions more migrants thread perilous paths through the Johnsongrass and *saguaro* cactus over the next few years. "You've got people running around down there with guns, thinking the sheriff's in support of what they're doing," says John Fife, who runs a Tucson-based group called Samaritan Patrol. "It's straight out of the Old West. When you get that kind of mindset, with this kind of immigration crisis, you've got all the potential for trouble. Real trouble."

A History of Torture

Trouble—real trouble—is nothing new in these parts. Ask anybody north or south of the border, and chances are they can tell you: Cochise County has a hard-earned reputation for racist violence.

That rep was cemented on a hot August day in 1976. Three Mexican nationals scaled the border fence into Cochise County, headed for nearby job sites. When they stopped to refill their water jug at a windmill, they were taken hostage at pistol-point by young rancher Tom Hanigan, who was soon joined by his brother, Patrick, and his elderly father, George, a right-wing political activist. According to attorney Antonio Bustamante and Tom Miller's book *On the Border,* the Mexican men were told, "All right, you f——ing wetbacks. You're not going anywhere."

While George Hanigan stood guard with his shotgun and guffawed, his boys hog-tied the Mexicans—later immortalized in folk song as *los tres mojados*—and used a knife to saw off their hair and strip off their clothes. The gringos built a mesquite fire near the naked migrants, burning their clothes and sacks of food while threatening and taunting the men. "Let's see if your Virgin of Guadalupe can help you now," George Hanigan sneered.

One of the Hanigan boys pulled a long iron out of the fire and dangled its hot end over the naked men's bodies. The other young Hanigan allegedly took it from him and touched it to one of the men's feet, again and again, until the stink of burning flesh mingled with the mesquite. The old man grabbed a knife and threatened to cut off one of the men's testicles. One of the men had a rope tied around his neck and was dragged through the scorching desert sand.

"When they'd had their fun," recalls long-time community activist Max Torres, "they cut them free one at a time, pointing them to Mexico and opening fire with birdshot." One of the men ended up with a back full of 47 pellets; another had 125. "Imagine the horror of the two remaining—and then the one remaining—as they heard the shots," Torres says.

Miraculously enough, *los tres mojados* survived to tell officials about their ordeal. Even more miraculously, the Cochise County attorney indicted the Hanigans on 11 counts each. Then the miracles ran out. George Hanigan died before the trial—but that only meant that he didn't live to be exonerated. An all-white jury of their Cochise County peers found Tom and Pat Hanigan not guilty of every charge.

For the next two decades, vigilantism broke out sporadically in Southeast Arizona. Sometimes the outlaws were local ranchers, like the one in 1980 who chained a 16-year-old Mexican immigrant by the neck to an outhouse toilet, torturing and starving him for four days.

Sometimes they were outside agitators like Civil Materiel Assistance, a paramilitary group that was also mixed up with the contras in Nicaragua. In 1986, CMA reportedly detained immigrants at gunpoint and later turned them over to Border Patrol agents, after having "had their fun" with the captives for hours.

But it was the Hanigan episode that let migrants know, once and for all, what could happen if they crossed into Cochise County. And now that the United States' hugely expensive "Southwest Border Initiative" has ensured that hundreds of thousands cross the border here every year, the memory of *los tres mojados* hangs over this desert like a bad dream.

Scariest of all, in many ways, was the way law-enforcement officials reacted. The Hanigans' only mistake, a couple of them told Tom Miller, was not finishing off the Mexicans. "I can see shooting them, you know, blowing their heads off," said Drex Atkinson, then a senior Border Patrol agent. "But torturing them makes no sense.". . .

"Evangelist of Fear"

Heading south from Red Rock, as Highway 80 snakes toward the border, there's a billboard you can't miss. Partly because there aren't many billboards in Cochise County. But mostly because this one features a gaggle of bigger-than-life gunfighters, aiming their weapons right at you. "O.K. Corral," reads the legend beneath the snarling outlaws, "Gunfights Daily!"

It's just a few miles farther on to Tombstone, where the most famous of Wild West shoot-outs gets re-enacted every day—and where, on a Wednesday afternoon in early December, the man who fired off the infamous call to arms in the

Tombstone Tumbleweed is sitting in his office. Chris Simcox's faithful .45 lies within arm's reach on his paper-strewn desk. And man, is he psyched.

"I have 600 people from everywhere in this country saying enough is enough," Simcox says in his high-pitched, rapid-fire voice. "It's grown beyond my wildest expectations. We've had 1,384 E-mails in support, let alone letters."

Simcox, a baby-faced 42-year-old who previously taught kindergarten in Los Angeles at a "very high-end, wealthy private school where I taught the kids of the stars and producers," moved to Tombstone in November 2001. He landed work as a hired gunslinger in Tombstone's daily shootouts and as a reporter for the *Tumbleweed,* which he bought when its previous owner decided to give up. In his spare time, Simcox says he began to patrol nearby Middlemarch Road, encountering "thousands" of migrants and apprehending 500.

Though he has been called an "evangelist of fear" by the Rev. Robin Hoover, who runs the Tucson-based humanitarian group Humane Borders, Simcox says there is nothing racist in his desire to round up immigrants. "I've got all the compassion in the world for them," he says.

So why raise a militia to stop them? Simcox first uses an economic argument, saying that unemployed U.S. citizens would love to have the low-wage jobs that many immigrants take. But his tune quickly changes. "I've lived in Manhattan and I have lived in Chicago and I've lived in Los Angeles. Those people don't come here to work. They come here to rob and deal drugs."

That's what drove him out of Los Angeles?

"Oh Jesus, it is unbelievable. I mean, we need the National Guard to clean out all our cities and round them up. They are hard-core criminals. They have no problem slitting your throat and taking your money or selling drugs to your kids or raping your daughters and they are evil people."

Adventure-Seekers

Simcox swears his intentions are peaceful. Civil Homeland Defense, the name he finally settled on for his group, will call the Border Patrol promptly after rounding up suspected illegal entrants. And their arsenal will be modest: "We will wear side-arms only, and even go to the point of no magnum loads," Simcox says.

None of which satisfies Mayor Dusty Escapule, a former deputy sheriff. "To me, there's only one reason you put a gun on and that is to kill somebody," says Escapule. "If their intentions are peaceful, well, take some blankets, water and sandwiches out to these people and say, 'Here's something to eat, here's some water, here's a warm coat or blanket if you want them, but we're gonna have to turn you over to the Border Patrol."

"I think they are adventure-seekers," agrees Douglas Mayor Ray Borane, who has gotten death threats for speaking out against vigilantism. "There's no danger involved for them. They are the ones packing the arms and looking important. There's no bravery there. There's no patriotism there. These people can't fight back and aren't gonna fight back; they're on their way to work. If the people *were* coming over here armed and they *were* fighting back, then we'd see how many volunteers he'd get."

The U.S. Border Patrol has no plans to monitor Simcox's group, according to spokesperson Ryan Scudder. But on Jan. 26 [2003], Simcox was arrested for possessing a loaded weapon, conducting a special operation without a permit and interfering with a law enforcement function in Coronado National Memorial, a park not far from Tombstone.

Simcox laughed off the incident, saying it would be "good publicity," but he told Glenn Spencer's Americanpatrol.com that the park ranger who cited him "mentioned her Hispanic heritage three times during the investigation." Picking up on this theme, the hate group California Coalition for Immigra-

Margulies. © by Jimmy Margulies. Reproduced by persmission.

tion Reform headlined a story on its Web site, "Chris Simcox Possibly Targeted by Latino Park Ranger."...

Gathering Storm

While the racial rhetoric and citizens' arrests continue to escalate, the number of migrants is set to swell to historic proportions as Mexico's shaky economy grows shakier still. Southern Arizonans got a taste of the coming catastrophe this past October [2002], traditionally the last month before the cold winds slow immigrant traffic to a relative trickle.

The Border Patrol nabbed twice as many illegal aliens as it did the previous October. Roger Barnett says he snared five times as many. Reports of citizens' arrests went up.

Unsolved shootings have also been on the rise. In early November, ... a masked man fired at a group of 14 immigrants southwest of Tucson, sending them scattering into the desert. On Feb. 12, a border-crosser was shot in the stomach in the same area—on the same day that shots were fired from a car at a group of six illegal entrants.

Nobody knows better than Mayor Escapule, whose town includes a bar featuring the "Tombstone Vigilantes Hall of Fame," that history dies hard in this part of the world—and that history indicates there's no end of nastiness on the horizon. But the subject perks up the burly, mustachioed mayor for a second, because there's something in the annals of Tombstone not nearly so well known as the gunfight at the O.K. Corral. Do you know, the mayor asks, what happened after the Earp boys turned Southeast Arizona into vigilante country?

"It was this way in Tombstone 120 years ago—you didn't know who the lawmen were," he says, settling back into his chair for a good yarn. "Not till a guy by the name of John Slaughter came in as Cochise County sheriff and showed them who the lawman was.

"Slaughter was 5-foot-2, they say, with steel-blue eyes. It's in the history books. And they say when Sheriff Slaughter went after his outlaw, if he didn't bring him back, he would bring back his boots.

"More often than not, he brought back the boots. But he stopped the vigilantism."

Who's going to stop it now?

Escapule grows uncharacteristically pensive. His mustache droops. Nowadays, he finally reckons, it would have to be the feds. "I think the U.S. government is gonna have to step in, say, 'Sorry, boys, you're out of line.'"

Unless that happens soon, the orneriest white guys in the West are about to get a lot more ornery—with agitators like . . . Simcox . . . egging them on.

"This is my land. I'm the victim here," [rancher] Roger Barnett recently growled in the right-wing *Washington Times*. Barnett, who says he's personally lobbied more than 300 members of Congress to do something about the border, knows it's

U.S. policy that's primarily responsible for victimizing him and his fellow ranchers. But he can't seem to make a dent in that.

He can make a dent in the migrant traffic, though. And with many thousands more headed right through his back yard, another thing Barnett told the *Times* was downright chilling. "Something has to be done or there's going to be bloodshed."

In this part of the world, a man's word is his bond.

Periodical Bibliography

The following articles have been selected to supplement the diverse views presented in this chapter.

Leslie Berestein   "Legislation and Media Raise the Temperature," *San Diego Union-Tribune*, May 13, 2005.

James Jay Carafano   "Border Security: Setting the Right Federal Priorities," Heritage Foundation, March 18, 2005.

Timothy P. Carney   "Open Borders, Closed Debate," *National Review Online*, September 1, 2004. www.national review.com.

Jon E. Dougherty   "New Military Branch: The United States Border Guard," *Sierra Times*, July 10, 2005.

Larry Elder   "Minutemen—Don't Call Us 'Vigilantes,'" *Jewish World Review*, April 14, 2005.

Daniel González and   "Illegal Immigration, It's Just Getting Worse,"
Susan Carroll   *Arizona Republic*, June 19, 2005.

Christopher Ketcham   "The Angry Patriot," May 11, 2005. www.salon .com.

Robert Locke   "The Open-Borders Conspiracy," July 15, 2002. www.frontpagemag.com.

Michelle Malkin   "What Part of 'Enforcement' Don't They Understand?" December 1, www.townhall.com.

Phyllis Schlafly   "What 9/11 Changed and Didn't Change," September 17, 2002. www.townhall.com.

Tom Tancredo   "Guest Workers, Yes! Amnesty, No!" *Human Events Online*, August 18, 2003. www.human eventsonline.com.

James A. Walsh   "Immigration Anarchists: Beyond Open Borders, What Do They Want?" December 21, 2004. www.newsmax.com.

Daniel B. Wood   "Past Has Cautionary Lessons for Guest Worker Programs," *Christian Science Monitor*, January 27, 2004.

CHAPTER 4

How Should U.S. Immigration Policy Be Reformed?

Chapter Preface

In December 2002 a man and woman were attacked while sitting on a bench near some railroad tracks in an isolated area of Queens, New York. The woman, a forty-two-year-old mother of two children, was abducted and brutally raped, and the man was severely beaten and robbed. The New York police arrested five men: four illegal aliens from Mexico, and one legal immigrant. Upon further investigation the media discovered that three of the illegal aliens had been arrested numerous times before on such charges as assault, attempted robbery, criminal trespass, illegal gun possession, and drug possession. Anti-immigration groups alleged that because of New York City's sanctuary policy, which leaves it to the police department's discretion whether to notify the U.S. Citizenship and Immigration Services (USCIS) about an individual's immigration status, these dangerous criminals had been let back out on the street instead of being deported under U.S. immigration law. The media were quick to point out that if the police had turned over these illegal immigrants to the USCIS the first time they had been arrested, the horrible crimes committed against the man and woman in Queens would never have happened.

Controversy erupted over sanctuary laws in large cities such as New York City and Los Angeles, which had enforced such policies for years. Supporters claimed that the sanctuary policies are beneficial to both immigrants and law enforcement. Because of these laws, immigrants do not have to worry about being deported if they are the victim or witness of a crime or unfairly charged with a crime. In addition, police officers do not have to function as immigration officers, a task for which they are not trained.

Opponents argue that by banning police officers from enforcing immigration laws, sanctuary policies are putting criminals back on the streets and endangering the community. They contend that identifying a suspect's immigration status is a valuable law-enforcement tool. Moreover, such policies leave law-abiding immigrants vulnerable to violence. In large urban areas young illegal aliens make up the majority of some street gangs and often terrorize neighborhoods populated by immigrants and their descendants.

Sanctuary laws are only one area of debate in America's ongoing efforts to reform its immigration policies. Others included in this chapter are whether amnesty should be granted to resident illegal aliens, the extent to which the United States should be cooperating with other countries on immigration issues, and the passage of the REAL ID Act.

> "*I propose a new temporary worker program that will match willing foreign workers with willing American employers.*"

Illegal Immigrant Workers Should Be Granted Legal Status

George W. Bush

In the following viewpoint George W. Bush, the president of the United States, outlines his proposals for reforming immigration laws. Bush argues that there are many jobs in America that U.S. citizens are unwilling to perform. Therefore, a temporary worker program is needed. Subject to strict controls, this program would grant temporary legal status to workers who are in the country illegally and would permit employers to recruit workers from other countries to fill their labor needs. Bush insists that this program would not be an amnesty for illegal immigrants because it would be temporary and closely regulated to ensure that immigrants either leave the country or follow the legal path to citizenship.

As you read, consider the following questions:

1. How have immigrants served the country, according to Bush?
2. What four principles should guide immigration reform,

George W. Bush, remarks on immigration policy, Washington, DC, January 17, 2004.

as listed by the author?

3. Why will his program help make the country more secure, according to Bush?

Many of you here today are Americans by choice, and you have followed in the path of millions. And over the generations we have received energetic, ambitious, optimistic people from every part of the world. By tradition and conviction, our country is a welcoming society. America is a stronger and better nation because of the hard work and the faith and entrepreneurial spirit of immigrants.

Every generation of immigrants has reaffirmed the wisdom of remaining open to the talents and dreams of the world. And every generation of immigrants has reaffirmed our ability to assimilate newcomers—which is one of the defining strengths of our country.

The Contributions of Immigrants

During one great period of immigration—between 1891 and 1920—our nation received some 18 million men, women and children from other nations. The hard work of these immigrants helped make our economy the largest in the world. The children of immigrants put on the uniform and helped to liberate the lands of their ancestors. One of the primary reasons America became a great power in the 20th century is because we welcomed the talent and the character and the patriotism of immigrant families.

The contributions of immigrants to America continue. About 14 percent of our nation's civilian workforce is foreign-born. Most begin their working lives in America by taking hard jobs and clocking long hours in important industries. Many immigrants also start businesses, taking the familiar path from hired labor to ownership.

As a Texan, I have known many immigrant families, mainly from Mexico, and I have seen what they add to our country.

They bring to America the values of faith in God, love of family, hard work and self reliance—the values that made us a great nation to begin with. We've all seen those values in action, through the service and sacrifice of more than 35,000 foreign-born men and women currently on active duty in the United States military. One of them is Master Gunnery Sergeant Guadalupe Denogean, an immigrant from Mexico who has served in the Marine Corps for 25 years and counting. Last year [2003], I was honored and proud to witness Sergeant Denogean take the oath of citizenship in a hospital where he was recovering from wounds he received in Iraq. I'm honored to be his Commander-in-Chief, I'm proud to call him a fellow American.

Laws Must Work

As a nation that values immigration, and depends on immigration, we should have immigration laws that work and make us proud. Yet today we do not. Instead, we see many employers turning to the illegal labor market. We see millions of hard-working men and women condemned to fear and insecurity in a massive, undocumented economy. Illegal entry across our borders makes more difficult the urgent task of securing the homeland. The system is not working. Our nation needs an immigration system that serves the American economy, and reflects the American Dream.

Reform must begin by confronting a basic fact of life and economics: some of the jobs being generated in America's growing economy are jobs American citizens are not filling. Yet these jobs represent a tremendous opportunity for workers from abroad who want to work and fulfill their duties as a husband or a wife, a son or a daughter.

Their search for a better life is one of the most basic desires of human beings. Many undocumented workers have walked mile after mile, through the heat of the day and the cold of the night. Some have risked their lives in dangerous

155

desert border crossings, or entrusted their lives to the brutal rings of heartless human smugglers. Workers who seek only to earn a living end up in the shadows of American life—fearful, often abused and exploited. When they are victimized by crime, they are afraid to call the police, or seek recourse in the legal system. They are cut off from their families far away, fearing if they leave our country to visit relatives back home, they might never be able to return to their jobs.

The situation I described is wrong. It is not the American way. Out of common sense and fairness, our laws should allow willing workers to enter our country and fill jobs that Americans are not filling. We must make our immigration laws more rational, and more humane. And I believe we can do so without jeopardizing the livelihoods of American citizens.

Controlling the Border

Our reforms should be guided by a few basic principles. First, America must control its borders. Following the attacks of September the 11th, 2001, this duty of the federal government has become even more urgent. And we're fulfilling that duty.

For the first time in our history, we have consolidated all border agencies under one roof to make sure they share information and the work is more effective. We're matching all visa applicants against an expanded screening list to identify terrorists and criminals and immigration violators. . . . We have begun using advanced technology to better record and track aliens who enter our country—and to make sure they leave as scheduled. We have deployed new gamma and x-ray systems to scan cargo and containers and shipments at ports of entry to America. We have significantly expanded the Border Patrol—with more than a thousand new agents on the borders, and 40 percent greater funding over the last two years. We're working closely with the Canadian and Mexican governments to increase border security. America is acting on a basic belief:

our borders should be open to legal travel and honest trade; our borders should be shut and barred tight to criminals, to drug traders, to drug traffickers and to criminals, and to terrorists.

Second, new immigration laws should serve the economic needs of our country. If an American employer is offering a job that American citizens are not willing to take, we ought to welcome into our country a person who will fill that job.

Third, we should not give unfair rewards to illegal immigrants in the citizenship process or disadvantage those who came here lawfully, or hope to do so.

Fourth, new laws should provide incentives for temporary, foreign workers to return permanently to their home countries after their period of work in the United States has expired.

Today, I ask the Congress to join me in passing new immigration laws that reflect these principles, that meet America's economic needs, and live up to our highest ideals.

A Temporary Worker Program

I propose a new temporary worker program that will match willing foreign workers with willing American employers, when no Americans can be found to fill the jobs. This program will offer legal status, as temporary workers, to the millions of undocumented men and women now employed in the United States, and to those in foreign countries who seek to participate in the program and have been offered employment here. This new system should be clear and efficient, so employers are able to find workers quickly and simply.

All who participate in the temporary worker program must have a job, or, if not living in the United States, a job offer. The legal status granted by this program will last three years and will be renewable—but it will have an end. Participants who do not remain employed, who do not follow the rules of the program, or who break the law will not be eligible

Not an Amnesty

Unlike our current immigration quotas, which are so unrealistic as to be unenforceable, a more honest, market-based system offers the only hope of restoring the rule of law—and that's not possible without a one-time transitional measure to eliminate the underground economy. Immigration skeptics can call it anything they like. But it's hard to see how "amnesty"—with all its connotations of laxity and lawlessness—is the right word to describe such a demanding bargain.

Tamar Jacoby, Wall Street Journal, *June 20, 2005.*

for continued participation and will be required to return to their home.

Under my proposal, employers have key responsibilities. Employers who extend job offers must first make every reasonable effort to find an American worker for the job at hand. Our government will develop a quick and simple system for employers to search for American workers. Employers must not hire undocumented aliens or temporary workers whose legal status has expired. They must report to the government the temporary workers they hire, and who leave their employ, so that we can keep track of people in the program, and better enforce immigration laws. There must be strong workplace enforcement with tough penalties for anyone, for any employer violating these laws.

Undocumented workers now here will be required to pay a one-time fee to register for the temporary worker program. Those who seek to join the program from abroad, and have complied with our immigration laws, will not have to pay any fee. All participants will be issued a temporary worker card that will allow them to travel back and forth between their home and the United States without fear of being denied re-entry into our country.

This program expects temporary workers to return perma-nently to their home countries after their period of work in the United States has expired. And there should be financial incentives for them to do so. I will work with foreign govern-ments on a plan to give temporary workers credit, when they enter their own nation's retirement system, for the time they have worked in America. I also support making it easier for temporary workers to contribute a portion of their earnings to tax-preferred savings accounts, money they can collect as they return to their native countries. After all, in many of those countries, a small nest egg is what is necessary to start their own business, or buy some land for their family.

No Amnesty

Some temporary workers will make the decision to pursue American citizenship. Those who make this choice will be al-lowed to apply in the normal way. They will not be given un-fair advantage over people who have followed legal procedures from the start. I oppose amnesty, placing undocumented workers on the automatic path to citizenship. Granting am-nesty encourages the violation of our laws, and perpetuates il-legal immigration. America is a welcoming country, but citi-zenship must not be the automatic reward for violating the laws of America.

The citizenship line, however, is too long, and our current limits on legal immigration are too low. My administration will work with the Congress to increase the annual number of green cards that can lead to citizenship. Those willing to take the difficult path of citizenship—the path of work, and pa-tience, and assimilation—should be welcome in America, like generations of immigrants before them.

In the process of immigration reform, we must also set high expectations for what new citizens should know. An understanding of what it means to be an American is not a formality in the naturalization process, it is essential to full participation in our democracy. My administration will examine the standard of knowledge in the current citizenship test. We must ensure that new citizens know not only the facts of our history, but the ideals that have shaped our history. Every citizen of America has an obligation to learn the values that make us one nation: liberty and civic responsibility, equality under God, and tolerance for others.

Security and Compassion

This new temporary worker program will bring more than economic benefits to America. Our homeland will be more secure when we can better account for those who enter our country, instead of the current situation in which millions of people are unknown, unknown to the law. Law enforcement will face fewer problems with undocumented workers, and will be better able to focus on the true threats to our nation from criminals and terrorists. And when temporary workers can travel legally and freely, there will be more efficient management of our borders and more effective enforcement against those who pose a danger to our country.

This new system will be more compassionate. Decent, hard-working people will now be protected by labor laws, with the right to change jobs, earn fair wages, and enjoy the same working conditions that the law requires for American workers. Temporary workers will be able to establish their identities by obtaining the legal documents we all take for granted. And they will be able to talk openly to authorities, to report crimes when they are harmed, without the fear of being deported.

The best way, in the long run, to reduce the pressures that create illegal immigration in the first place is to expand economic opportunity among the countries in our neighborhood. In a few days I will go to Mexico for the Special Summit of the Americas, where we will discuss ways to advance free trade, and to fight corruption, and encourage the reforms that lead to prosperity. Real growth and real hope in the nations of our hemisphere will lessen the flow of new immigrants to America when more citizens of other countries are able to achieve their dreams at their own home.

Yet our country has always benefited from the dreams that others have brought here. By working hard for a better life, immigrants contribute to the life of our nation. The temporary worker program I am proposing today represents the best tradition of our society, a society that honors the law, and welcomes the newcomer. This plan will help return order and fairness to our immigration system, and in so doing we will honor our values, by showing our respect for those who work hard and share in the ideals of America.

"The Bush administration has been torturing the English language in an effort to craft a new amnesty for millions of illegal aliens without saying the dreaded word: 'amnesty.'"

Illegal Immigrants Should Not Be Granted Legal Status

William F. Jasper

In January 2004 President George W. Bush outlined his plan for reforming the nation's immigration laws. Among his proposals was a guest worker program that would grant legal status to immigrant workers who were in the country illegally and invite additional workers from abroad. In the following viewpoint William F. Jasper criticizes this plan on the grounds that it amounts to an amnesty for lawbreakers and will lead to a large increase in the number of people crossing the borders illegally. Jasper is the senior editor of the New American, *a conservative magazine.*

As you read, consider the following questions:

1. How did former Homeland Security secretary Tom Ridge broach the topic of amnesty, as reported by Jasper?

2. In the author's view, why do many conservatives back Bush's plan when they opposed President Clinton's?

3. What are Bush's views on amnesty, according to the author?

Get ready for a battle royale to save our borders. The Bush administration and pro-immigration invasion Democrats and Republicans in Congress are planning a big move ... to give amnesty to millions of illegal aliens now residing in the United States. President Bush and his counterpart in Mexico, President Vicente Fox, were forced to put this scheme on hold in 2001, following the 9/11 terrorist attacks. Now the plan is back, along with a multitude of connected initiatives to deluge the U.S. with waves of legal immigrants, "refugees," "temporary workers" and your standard variety of illegal alien border jumpers.

Republicans and conservatives maintained a continuous cannonade against President Clinton for his blatant disregard of our borders and his efforts to swell the Democrat Party's voting ranks by giving citizenship to hundreds of thousands of illegal aliens. Continuing these policies, they warned, would lead to national suicide. Many of those voices, however, have been strangely mute as President Bush has continued, and in some cases expanded, Clinton's suicidal immigration policies. Some have actually switched from jeering to cheering, apparently convinced that any policy, no matter how bankrupt, destructive or unconstitutional, suddenly becomes beneficial when backed by Republican Party leadership.

Sending Up Signals

The Bush administration sent some important signals on this front in December [2003]. First, Homeland Security Secretary Tom Ridge sent up a flare at a December 9 town hall–style meeting at Miami Dade College. A Copley News Service report of the event on December 11 made the following observation:

> In the strongest sign to date that the Bush administration is considering a major immigration initiative next year, Homeland Security Secretary Tom Ridge has called for "some kind of legal status" for the estimated 8 million to 12 million immigrants living illegally in the United States.

Ridge, who oversees the nation's borders, also said that such an unprecedented legalization program should be coupled with a decision about "what our immigration policy is," followed by a firm commitment to enforce it.

What does the Bush legalization process mean? "I'm not saying make them citizens, because they violated the law to get here," Ridge said at the Miami event. "You determine how you can legalize their presence. Then, as a country, you make a decision that from this day forward . . . this is the process of entry, and if you violate that process of entry we have the resources to cope with it."

Amnesty Disaster Replay

Legalize their presence but never allow them to become citizens? Does this mean that they would become permanent legal aliens? Mr. Ridge knows that is an absurd notion; once the millions of illegals are legalized, the political pressure will build inexorably to grant them full citizenship.

And what of Secretary Ridge's talk about getting tough "from this day forward"—meaning after the legalization? "We've heard that one before," says Karl Nelson, a retired investigator for the former Immigration and Naturalization Service (INS). "Look, that's what the immigration 'reformers' promised with the 1986 IRCA [Immigration Reform and Control Act] amnesty," Nelson told *The New American.* "But what really happened? Most of INS resources were shifted over to processing nearly three million aliens for amnesty. Did we get the promised enforcement increases? No. Did that amnesty satisfy the amnesty advocates? No. They immediately pushed for widening the amnesty and granting innumerable exceptions. And the [Reagan-Bush] administration caved in. Did we get control of our borders as promised? No. As everyone should know by now, our borders continued to be overrun— and still are being overrun. Show me one reason why we should trust in the new promises when the record shows that all similar promises in the past have been broken."

The new Bush amnesty would be far worse than previous amnesties, says Nelson, who served 25 years in the Border Patrol and INS. "The paperwork alone will be a killer," he notes. "The IRCA amnesty program ate up much of the INS budget and tied up an extraordinary percentage of INS personnel. How will they process several times that number of applicants? The reality is that lightening budgets together with personnel overload and political pressure to speed the process will result in rubberstamping not only millions of current illegal residents, but millions more who will come to take advantage of the opportunity. Besides all of the usual economic and social problems this will cause an incredible security problem. Homeland security? This is absolutely ludicrous."

Rep. Tom Tancredo (R-Colo.), a leading congressional champion of immigration control, was likewise appalled. "I can think of few things that could be more dangerous for homeland security than granting amnesty to 8 to 12 million illegal aliens," said Rep. Tancredo, in response to Secretary Ridge's remarks. "Perhaps the administration ought to dedicate more energy to enforcing our existing immigration laws and less on finding ways to allow millions to skirt them."

White House Spin Cycle

At a December 11[2003] press briefing, White House spokesman Scott McClellan was asked if Secretary Ridge's statements were signaling a new amnesty policy. Mr. McClellan said "no," but acknowledged "there are some that had interpreted this as some broad amnesty discussion, and that's not at all what he was suggesting." However, McClellan then failed to offer anything that would dispel the alleged misinterpretation. In a muddled and evasive explanation, he stated that Ridge has been "looking at the issue of the large number of illegal immigrants we do have in the country, and looking at those that could be threats and those that are here for other reasons.

And so he's just talking about the realities that we are facing now."

A few days later, at a December 15 press conference, President Bush told reporters that he "is firmly against blanket amnesty." This is more of the Clintonian rhetorical slithering we've come to expect on this issue. Note the president didn't say "no amnesty," just no "blanket amnesty." Bush's upcoming selective amnesty (or amnesties) is apparently intended to look conservative compared to one that unreservedly proclaims amnesty for all illegal aliens regardless of nationality or circumstances.

At the same press conference, President Bush made another important statement. He declared: "I have constantly said that we need to have an immigration policy that helps match any willing employer with any willing employee." The president has indeed repeatedly expressed this policy position and done everything possible to implement it. What is extraordinary is that this radical position has gone largely unexamined and uncontested by conservative and liberal-left politicos and commentators alike. There are literally hundreds of millions of "willing employees" throughout the world who would gladly come here to work for a fraction of what American employees are paid. If President Bush's immigration policy is being framed, as he himself has repeatedly said, to "match any willing employer with any willing employee," then we are in for a continuous immigration deluge—and a huge rise in layoffs of American citizens, as their jobs are taken by willing foreign employees.

Amnesty by Any Other Name

Back in September 2001, *The New American* observed regarding the Bush-Fox amnesty threat: "The Bush administration has been torturing the English language in an effort to craft a new amnesty for millions of illegal aliens without saying the dreaded word: 'amnesty.' Some newly devised euphemisms in-

Wright. © 2005 by Copley News Service. Reproduced by permission.

clude 'regularization,' 'legalization,' 'permanent status,' and 'earned adjustment.' President Bush has repeatedly dodged the amnesty issue, refusing to use the term. Still, when recently pressed on the issue, he insisted that his soon-to-be-revealed immigration policy vis-à-vis Mexico will not include a 'blanket amnesty.'"

We noted that "whatever Clintonesque term is finally adopted as the cover for the Bush policy, a large amnesty is certain to be the central component of his immigration package." And it is coming, regardless of the intentionally conflicting signals being sent by the White House. As the Copley News Service reported on December 11, 2003, "the administration is considering a major election-year immigration initiative." The report continued:

> In September, Sen. Larry Craig, R-Idaho, said he had received White House assurances that if a bill he drafted to legalize between 500,000 and 800,000 farm workers reached the president's desk, Bush would sign it. . . .

And [in January 2004], Rep. Jeff Flake, R-Ariz., said in an interview that Karl Rove, Bush's chief political strategist, promised a presidential push to deliver on immigration reforms sought by Mexican President Vicente Fox and advocates for undocumented workers.

The Rove-Bush strategy aims at keeping the Republican core distracted with other matters until the administration has put together a sufficiently impressive coalition of business leaders and radical Hispanic militants as to appear unstoppable. The Bush White House then intends to ram its amnesty plan through Congress before opponents can rally to stop it.

┃ *"The evidence for the destructive effects*
┃ *of sanctuary laws is clear."*

Sanctuary Policies Should Be Abolished

Heather Mac Donald

Many cities have sanctuary policies that prohibit police from reporting the immigration status of criminal suspects to immigration officials. In the following viewpoint Heather Mac Donald argues that sanctuary policies allow dangerous illegal immigrant criminals to remain on the streets and commit multiple crimes. She maintains that abolishing sanctuary policies will reduce the gang violence problem that devastates some urban areas. Mac Donald is an author and a senior fellow at the Manhattan Institute for Policy Research, a think tank in New York City. She has analyzed the issue of illegal immigration for City Journal *and the* Los Angeles Times.

As you read, consider the following questions:

1. According to recent estimates, how many gang members are illegal aliens?

2. How has Los Angeles recently changed its sanctuary law, according to the author, and why is this change insufficient?

3. How does Mac Donald respond to the argument that sanctuary laws are pro-immigrant?

Heather Mac Donald, testimony before the U.S. House Subcommittee on Immigration, Border Security and Claims, Committee on the Judiciary, Washington, DC, April 13, 2005.

Sanctuary laws are a serious impediment to stemming gang violence and other crime. Moreover, they are a perfect symbol of this country's topsy-turvy stance towards illegal immigration.

Sanctuary laws, present in such cities as Los Angeles, New York, Chicago, Austin, Houston, and San Francisco, generally forbid local police officers from inquiring into a suspect's immigration status or reporting it to federal authorities. Such laws place a higher priority on protecting illegal aliens from deportation than on protecting legal immigrants and citizens from assault, rape, arson, and other crimes.

Let's say a Los Angeles police officer sees a member of Mara Salvatrucha hanging out at Hollywood and Vine. The gang member has previously been deported for aggravated assault; his mere presence back in the country following deportation is a federal felony. Under the prevailing understanding of Los Angeles's sanctuary law (special order 40), if that officer merely inquires into the gangbanger's immigration status, the officer will face departmental punishment.

To get the felon off the street, the cop has to wait until he has probable cause to arrest the gangbanger for a non-immigration crime, such as murder or robbery. It is by no means certain that that officer *will* successfully build a non-immigrant case against the gangster, however, since witnesses to gang crime often fear deadly retaliation if they cooperate with the police. Meanwhile, the gangbanger is free to prey on law-abiding members of his community, many of them immigrants themselves.

An Inefficient Approach

This is an extraordinary inefficient way to reduce crime. If an officer has grounds for arresting a criminal now, it is perverse to ask him to wait until some later date when maybe, if he is lucky, he will have an additional ground for arrest.

Sanctuary laws violate everything we have learned about policing in the 1990s. Police departments across the country discovered that utilizing every law enforcement tool in their tool chest against criminals yielded enormous gains. Getting criminals off the streets for seemingly "minor" crimes such as turnstile jumping or graffiti saved lives. Gang crime, which exploded 50% from 1999 to 2002, is too serious a problem to ignore this lesson.

Illegals and Gangs

No one knows for certain the percentage of illegals in gangs, thanks in large part to sanctuary laws themselves. But various estimates exist:

—A confidential California Department of Justice study reported in 1995 that 60 percent of the 20,000-strong 18th Street Gang in southern California is illegal; police officers say the proportion is actually much greater. The bloody gang collaborates with the Mexican Mafia, the dominant force in California prisons, on complex drug-distribution schemes, extortion, and drive-by assassinations. It commits an assault or robbery every day in L.A. County. The gang has grown dramatically over the last two decades by recruiting recently arrived youngsters, most of them illegal, from Central America and Mexico.

—Immigration and Customs Enforcement conservatively puts the number of illegals in Mara Salvatrucha as a "majority"; police officers, by contrast, assert that the gang is overwhelmingly illegal.

—Law enforcement officials estimate that 20% of gang members in San Diego County are illegal, according to the *Union-Tribune.*

—The L.A. County Sheriff reported in 2000 that 23% of inmates in county jails were deportable, according to the *New York Times.*

—The leadership of the Columbia Lil' Cycos gang, which

uses murder and racketeering to control the drug market around Los Angeles's MacArthur Park, was about 60 percent illegal in 2002. Francisco Martinez, a Mexican Mafia member and an illegal alien, controlled the gang from prison, while serving time for felonious reentry following deportation.

—In Los Angeles, 95 percent of all outstanding warrants for homicide in the first half of 2004 (which totaled 1,200 to 1,500) targeted illegal aliens. Up to two-thirds of all fugitive felony warrants (17,000) were for illegal aliens.

—The Los Angeles Police Department arrests about 2500 criminally-convicted deportees annually, reports the *Los Angeles Times*.

The Destructive Effects of Sanctuary

Though the numbers of illegal gang members remain elusive, the evidence for the destructive effects of sanctuary laws is incontrovertible. In 2002, for example, four illegal Mexicans, accompanied by one legal immigrant, abducted and brutally raped a 42-year-old mother of two near some railroad tracks in Queens, New York. The New York Police Department had already arrested three of the illegal aliens numerous times for such crimes as assault, attempted robbery, criminal trespass, illegal gun possession, and drug offenses. But pursuant to New York's sanctuary policy, the department had never notified the INS.

Five months ago [November 2004], Carlos Barrera, an illegal Mexican in Hollywood, Ca., mugged three people, burglarized two apartments, and tried to rape a five-year-old girl. Barrera had been deported four years ago after serving time for robbery, drugs, and burglary. Since his reentry following deportation, he had been stopped twice for traffic violations.

A Topsy-Turvy Immigration Environment

However pernicious in themselves, sanctuary rules are a symptom of a much broader disease: the nation's near-total loss of control over immigration policy. Fifty years ago, immigration policy might have driven immigration numbers, but today the numbers drive policy. The nonstop increase of immigration is reshaping the language and the law to dissolve any distinction between legal and illegal aliens and, ultimately, the very idea of national borders.

It is a measure of how topsy-turvy the immigration environment has become that to ask police officials about the illegal-alien crime problem feels like a gross faux pas, not done in polite company. And a police official asked to violate this powerful taboo will give a strangled response—or, as in the case of a New York deputy commissioner, break off communication altogether. Meanwhile, millions of illegal aliens work, shop, travel, and commit crimes in plain view, utterly secure in their de facto immunity from the immigration law.

Heather Mac Donald, City Journal, *Winter 2004.*

But thanks to special order 40, the police had never mentioned him to the immigration authorities, reports the *New York Times.*

In September, 2003, the Miami police arrested a Honduran visa violator for seven vicious rapes. The previous year, Miami cops had had the suspect in custody for lewd and lascivious molestation. Pursuant to Miami's sanctuary law, however, the police had never checked his immigration status. Had they done so, they would have discovered his deportable status, and could have forestalled the rapes.

Cousins Aneceto and Jaime Reyes committed murder and a car-jacking, respectively, after returning to Los Angeles from

Mexico following deportation. The Los Angeles police had encountered them before these most recent crimes, but had to wait for them to commit murder and a car-jacking before they could lay a finger on them for their immigration offenses, according to the *New York Times*.

Sanctuary Policies in Los Angeles

The Los Angeles Police Department began revisiting special order 40 last month [March 2005]. Its proposed revision merely underlines how perverse our attitudes towards illegal alien criminals remain.

Los Angeles's top brass propose to allow a Los Angeles officer who suspects that a criminal has previously been deported to contact his supervisor about the reentry felony. That supervisor would then contact ICE [Immigration and Customs Enforcement]. ICE officials would next go before a federal judge to get an arrest warrant for the immigration felony. Then, with warrant in hand, the Los Angeles cop may finally arrest the felonious gangbanger—if he can still find him.

This burdensome procedure is preposterous. To arrest an American citizen for a crime, arrest warrants are rarely required; about 95% of arrests of citizens are warrantless. But in L.A., under the new rules, illegal criminals will have due process rights that citizens can only dream of: not just judicial review before they can be taken off the streets, but *federal* judicial review—the gold standard of all constitutional protections. Maybe homegrown criminals should renounce their citizenship and reenter the country illegally. It would be a constitutional windfall for them.

Limiting Law Enforcement

Other jurisdictions that are reconsidering their sanctuary laws are also proceeding with unnecessary timidity. The Orange County, Ca., sheriff plans to train a few deputies to use immigration laws only for special enforcement actions against sexual predators or gangs, reports the *Los Angeles Times*. The

Miami Police Department will join with ICE only on high-level gang cases.

These minor tinkerings all put unwise limitations on a vital law enforcement power. Local immigration enforcement power should not be limited to the felony of reentry following deportation. Nor should only a small subset of officers be authorized to use it. There are many illegal alien criminals who have not yet reentered following deportation, but who are just as dangerous to their communities. Every officer should have the power to enforce any immigration violation against a criminal suspect, not just immigration felonies.

Nothing demonstrates the necessity of this power better than ICE's March [2005] enforcement action against Mara Salvatrucha. Following the March round-up, ICE proudly displayed three of its trophy cases: the founding member of MS-13 in Hollywood, Ca., who had already been convicted for robbery and possession of a dangerous weapon; the leader of MS-13 in Long Branch, NJ, who had a prior criminal history of aggravated arson, weapons possession, grand larceny, and criminal possession of stolen property; and the founder of Port Washington, NY's, MS gang, who had a prior drug conviction.

ICE got all three of these leading gang bangers off the streets through what it calls administrative immigration violations, not felony immigration violations. Local officers in Hollywood, Long Branch, and Port Washington, as elsewhere, should have the power to use any type of immigration violation as well to get a thug (who may also prove to be a terrorist) off the street.

Empower Law Enforcement

Immigration enforcement against criminals should also not wait upon a major federal-local gang initiative. The majority of opportunities to get criminals off the streets come from enforcing misdemeanors and quality of life offenses. While the police are waiting to make a major federal case against an illegal criminal, they are far more likely to have picked him up for a "petty" theft or an open-container offense. Officers should be empowered at every arrest or lawful stop to check someone's immigration status. If a suspect is committing an immigration offense, the officer should be empowered to arrest him immediately for that offense.

Jails and prisons should routinely check the immigration status of their prisoners. Such an initiative should not be dependent on the presence of an ICE officer stationed in a prison; there are simply not enough federal agents available to cover the relevant facilities. Moreover, ICE agents do not routinely visit local jails where misdemeanor offenders are held, yet those offenders may be as dangerous to the community as someone against whom a felony case has been made. Someone convicted of stealing a jacket today may be shooting a rival tomorrow. And many misdemeanor convicts in jails have been allowed to plead down from more serious felonies.

The standard argument for sanctuary laws is that they encourage illegal aliens to work with the police or seek government services. This argument is based on myth, not evidence. No illegal alien advocate has ever provided a shred of evidence that sanctuary laws actually accomplish their alleged ends. Nor has anyone shown that illegal aliens are even aware of sanctuary laws. The evidence for the destructive effects of sanctuary laws is clear, however.

The idea that sanctuary laws are "pro-immigrant" is perhaps the greatest myth of all. Keeping illegal criminals in the community subjects all immigrants to the thrall of crime and impedes economic growth in immigrant communities.

Obviously, the final prerequisite for ridding immigrant communities of illegal thugs is enough ICE detention space and deportation resources. But providing police officers with every lawful tool to fight crime is a crucial first step to protecting immigrant lives.

> "Local law enforcement officials do not have the training and expertise that is necessary to determine who is presently lawfully in the country."

Sanctuary Policies Should Not Be Abolished

Sheila Jackson Lee

Sheila Jackson Lee is a Democratic congresswoman from Texas. In the following viewpoint she responds to criticism of a New York policy that prohibits local police from reporting immigration violations to immigration officials. This type of law, often called a sanctuary policy, has been criticized for impeding the efforts of police. Lee rejects this assertion. She contends that such laws contain exceptions that allow police to report the immigration status of suspects in certain situations. In addition, she asserts that allowing police to enforce immigration law would harm relations between police and immigrant communities.

As you read, consider the following questions:

1. What is New York Executive Order no. 124, as explained by the author?
2. Why is it important for police to develop strong ties to the immigrant community, in Lee's opinion?
3. How have immigrants been victimized by criminals, according to the author?

Sheila Jackson Lee, address to the U.S. House Committee on the Judiciary, February 27, 2003.

This morning [February 27, 2003] . . . we are pursuing an issue that needs addressing. And certainly, we are told of accounts, many accounts, that deal with immigrant issues and the criminal system.

In particular, we are aware of an incident that occurred in New York—Queens, New York, in particular—that an alleged group of young and homeless men surrounded a couple sitting on a bench in an isolated part of Queens, New York. And the allegations of a criminal incident that occurred where they beat and robbed the man and raped the woman.

Apparently, it was alleged that four of the men were undocumented aliens from Mexico who had been arrested previously.

One of the questions for this hearing, as was stated, is whether a New York City policy prevented the police involved in the previous arrest from reporting the men to the Immigration and Naturalization Service.

What Is Executive Order 124?

The policy in question is set forth in Executive Order No. 124, which was issued by New York Mayor Ed Koch on August 7, 1989. It is entitled, "City Policy Concerning Aliens."

This order prohibits the transmission of information about an alien to the Immigration Service. But the prohibition has three exceptions, one of which is for the situation in which the alien is suspected of engaging in criminal activity. And I repeat that again. There is an exception. The police did have discretion.

This order, therefore, did not prevent the police from reporting the homeless men to the Immigration Service when they were arrested previously. The pertinent issue regarding that case is whether the New York Police Department should have been required by Federal law to report the homeless men to the Immigration Service.

I believe it is imperative to assess the challenges that local police have. They have enormous challenges. And so the question is whether or not you add to them the responsibility of enforcing immigration law.

But when we ask that question, we have to look to the issue of whether or not, by definition, immigration equates to either terrorism or criminal activity.

I think the statistics would prove that that is not the case, so discretion is appropriate. That means that when there is suggestion of criminal activity, when there is any activity—whether it be misdemeanor level or otherwise—and they are engaged in a criminal activity, discretion does come about.

We have to realize that our immigrants do many things. They work for us. They live in our communities. They provide police officers with insight and information about criminal activity going on in their particular communities. They speak, sometimes, two languages. If they've learned the English language, which they will and eventually do, and therefore are able to provide information because they are bilingual or maybe even multilingual.

Immigration law is a complicated body of law that requires extensive training and expertise. It is also not a body of only criminal law or criminal law at all. It is a civilian body of law. It is a law that deals with immigrants accessing the process of citizenship.

Local law enforcement officials do not have the training and expertise that is necessary to determine who is presently lawfully in the country and who is not.

Community-Based Policing

Community-based policing is one of the most powerful law enforcement tools available. I know for a fact that it is utilized in New York. I know for a fact it is utilized in Houston. It is effective.

Defending Sanctuary Policies

There are times when undocumented aliens must have a substantial degree of protection. For example, parents fearful of having their family deported may very well not send their children to public schools. That could mean that a potential 70,000 to 80,000 undocumented children might remain hidden in apartments or be turned out on the streets. And some of these children are citizens—born in the U.S.— even though their parents were not.

If their parents take them out of school, not only will these children suffer irreversible damage, they will most likely end up doing damage to the rest of society. Similarly, illegal and undocumented immigrants should be able to seek medical help without the threat of being reported. When these people are sick, they're just as sick and just as contagious as citizens . . . and could possibly become a danger to public health.

And everyone should understand the practicality of wanting undocumented immigrants to feel comfortable reporting criminals to the police. Reporting criminals protects all people, citizens and non-citizens alike. It makes absolutely no sense to create a disincentive for immigrants to report crimes. Muggers don't ask for a green card. The federal government should not mandate state and city policies that have the effect of reducing the number of undocumented aliens reporting crimes.

Rudolph Giuliani, speech at the Kennedy School of Government, Harvard University, October 10, 1996.

Police get to understand and know the community, and people, by their very nature of wanting to be law-abiding—no matter who they are, immigrant or citizen—come to respect and admire the police and provide them with information to help them solve cases and problems.

By developing strong ties with local communities, police departments are able to obtain valuable information that helps them to fight a crime, even in a bilingual immigrant community or a single-language immigrant community. The development of community-based policing has been widely recognized as an effective tool for keeping kids off drugs, combating gang violence, and reducing crime rates in neighborhoods around the country.

In immigrant communities, it is particularly difficult for the police to establish the relationships that are the foundations for such successful police work. Many immigrants come from countries in which people are afraid of police who may be corrupt or even violent, and the prospect of being reported to the Immigration Service would be further reason for distrusting the police here in the United States of America.

In some cities, criminals have exploited the fear that immigrant communities have of all law enforcement officials, and certainly that should not be the case. For instance, in Durham, North Carolina, thieves told their victims in a community of migrant workers and new immigrants that if they called the police they would be deported, and they may be—may have been under legitimate agricultural visas and provisions to be in this Country.

Local police officers have found that people are being robbed multiple times and are not reporting the crimes because of such fear instilled by robbers. These immigrants are left vulnerable to crimes of all sorts, not just robbery.

In 1998, Elena Gonzalez, an immigrant in New Jersey, was found murdered in the basement of her apartment. Friends of the woman said that the suspected murderer, her former boyfriend, threatened to report her to the INS if she did not do what she was told.

We realize that there are sex slaves. There are young women who are brought into this country and held for months and years at a time, because I know that they are fearful of the police as well.

Use Resources Wisely

Many communities find it difficult financially to support a police force with the personnel and equipment necessary to perform regular police work. Requiring State and local police forces to report to the Immigration Service would be, I believe, an imbalanced, misdirected use of these limited resources.

Remember, it is important to note that the police have discretion, that as they encourage and become familiar and involved with the immigrant community, as the police forces are diversified with Hispanics, African Americans, Asians, individuals from the Muslim community, Arab community—those are individuals who are men and women who believe in upholding the law.

Let them become familiar with these neighborhoods, and I can assure you that crime will come down and problems will be solved.

The Immigration Service has limited resources, yes. But as we look toward this new year—the Homeland Security Department, the Justice Department—we know that we'll be refining these resources and adding training to these particular law enforcement agencies as we give more dollars to the first responders.

Let us be reminded of the terrible, horrific act of the snipers here in this region and the information that was important that was given to solve those problems by immigrants who were first allegedly targeted as the perpetrators, and it was not the case.

The Immigration Service does not have the resources it needs to deport dangerous criminals, prevent persons from unlawfully entering or remaining in the United States, and we must give them those resources. And we need to have the INS with the resources that it needs to enforce immigration laws in the interior of the country.

That is what we will be working on. That is an important responsibility, and that is a responsibility that I support.

Having to respond to every State and local police officer's report of someone who appears to be an illegal alien would prevent the Immigration Service from properly prioritizing its efforts and working to ensure that its major work of getting those dangerously in our Country deported would be delayed.

Local police can and should report immigrants to the Immigration Service in many situations. I encourage them to do so. With that kind of process and policy, we can work collectively together, keeping our responsibilities as a Federal Government and keeping our responsibilities to our local constituents in the work that the local official should be doing. The decision to contact Immigration Service, however, should be a matter of police discretion and not a Federal law decision.

| "The REAL ID Act is the only alternative to a national ID card."

The REAL ID Act Will Help Control Illegal Immigration

Mark Krikorian

In May 2005 President George W. Bush signed into law the REAL ID Act, which sets minimum federal requirements for state ID cards and driver's licenses. One goal of the act is to prevent illegal immigrants from obtaining driver's licenses or IDs that would confer the benefits of citizenship. In the following viewpoint Mark Krikorian argues that the REAL ID Act will help prevent terrorism by illegal immigrants. Krikorian is executive director of the Center for Immigration Studies (CIS) and a visiting fellow at the Nixon Center. He has written extensively on the subject of immigration policy.

As you read, consider the following questions:

1. How did the September 11, 2001, terrorist attacks highlight the need to better regulate IDs, according to the author?

2. What examples of problems with the issuance of improper IDs does Krikorian provide?

3. How might the REAL ID Act prevent the creation of a national ID card system, in Krikorian's opinion?

When Mexican President Vicente Fox visits President Bush's ranch ... [in March 2005] he is sure to complain about his host's support for the REAL ID Act, which effectively bans driver's licenses for illegal aliens. The House appended the measure ... to the supplemental appropriations bill for Iraq operations, guaranteeing a Senate debate on the issue. It's likely that there will be another showdown between the two houses of Congress like the one that took place ... over the intelligence reform bill. [The bill passed in the House and Senate and was signed into law on May 11, 2005.]

Originally approved by the House in February by a 100-vote margin (with only eight Republicans opposed), the REAL ID Act (H.R. 418) would, among other things, establish certain minimum standards for states if they want their driver's licenses or non-driver IDs to be accepted for federally mandated purposes, such as boarding a plane or entering a federal facility. The standards include verifying the legal status of the applicant, setting the license of a foreign visitor to expire when his visa expires, verifying documents presented by applicants, and modernizing the technology used in licenses.

Some libertarians have denounced the license requirements as the precursor to a national ID card. *The Wall Street Journal* helpfully invoked the Gestapo by decrying the bill's "show-us-your-papers" approach. Rep. Ron Paul (R., Tex.), God bless him, called the bill "a Soviet-style internal passport system." And the ACLU [American Civil Liberties Union] said it's "laying the foundation" for a national ID card.

Eternal vigilance is indeed the price of liberty, so extra sensitivity to proposals like the REAL ID Act is all to the good. But after a close look, it should be clear there is no national ID card lurking in this bill; after all, Phyllis Schlafly sure wouldn't support it if there were.

But there's more. It's not just that the bill wouldn't establish a national ID; by making our existing, decentralized iden-

REAL ID Will Protect the United States

While we did not prevent 9/11 from happening, the Real ID Act is vital to preventing foreign terrorists from hiding in plain sight while planning another attack just like it.

James Sensenbrenner, USA Today, May 9, 2005.

tification arrangements more secure, the REAL ID Act is the only thing that can stop a national ID card.

A Need for Stronger Measures

The need for more security in our existing document system was highlighted by the 9/11 Commission: "The federal government should set standards for the issuance of birth certificates and sources of identification, such as driver's licenses. Fraud in identification documents is no longer just a problem of theft. At many entry points to vulnerable facilities, including gates for boarding aircraft, sources of identification are the last opportunity to ensure that people are who they say they are and to check whether they are terrorists."

At least two of the 9/11 hijackers had overstayed their visas, and thus their state-issued IDs should have expired. As legal means of entry become increasingly difficult for terrorists, they will seek to enter illegally (as suggested by persistent intelligence reports), making access to government-issued IDs all the more important. In fact . . . the 9/11 Commission's counsel told the Senate Judiciary Committee of al Qaeda operative Nabil Al-Marabh, who sneaked illegally over the Canadian border in mid-2001 and was found to have received five Michigan licenses in 13 months, plus licenses from Massachusetts, Illinois, and Florida.

Nor is this laxity purely a Sept. 10 phenomenon; our state-based identification system remains in serious trouble. The

Coalition for a Secure Driver's License cleverly has ranked the states according to the Homeland Security Department's color-coding system, with too many states still in the red, "severe risk" category. Some continuing problems: Over the past six years, Utah has issued 56,498 driver licenses and 37,481 non-driver IDs to people without Social Security numbers—i.e. illegal aliens. In New York State, one Social Security number was used to get 57 driver's licenses. And . . . an illegal alien in Florida presented a driver's license so he could go to work—at *a nuclear power plant.*

After 9/11, calls for a national ID card were widespread; from 9/11 until the end of 2001, there were almost three times as many Nexis hits for "national ID" as there were for all of 2000. As the *Washington Post* wrote in December 2001, "Almost from the day the planes hit the World Trade Center and the Pentagon, members of Congress, security experts and high-tech executives have endorsed the idea of some new form of identification system as a critical weapon in the fight against terrorism."

An Attractive Alternative

In the wake of another attack the momentum could be politically irresistible, unless the public was satisfied that improvements to our existing system were already under way. And there might well be less resistance among lawmakers anyway, since most Democratic congressmen (and too many Republicans) don't really want the borders to be controlled in the first place; so the development of a federally issued universal ID would be an attractive alternative for politicians wanting to appear responsive to the Islamist threat.

Some of the bill's opponents seem especially out of touch. *The Wall Street Journal,* for instance, wrote, "It's not hard to imagine these de facto national ID cards turning into a kind of domestic passport that U.S. citizens would be asked to produce for everyday commercial and financial tasks." The *Journal's* editorial writers must not get out much, because regular people have been producing government-issued photo IDs "for everyday commercial and financial tasks" for a very long time. The choice is not between the minimum standards in the REAL ID Act, on the one hand, and on the other, some libertarian utopia where no one knows your name. The choice we are faced with is a tightening of our current, decentralized system of identification, or the eventual demand by a frightened public for a genuine, centralized national ID system.

This isn't the first time the libertarians have fought improvements in ID security. Congress in 1996 actually passed some minimal standards for licenses, but as the implementation deadline approached two years later, then-Rep. Bob Barr (R., Ga.) led the effort to kill the measure. And the president's initial 2002 border security proposal also had such standards in it, but they were pronounced dead on arrival by then Majority Leader Dick Armey (R., Tex.).

So once again, libertarian ideologues are objective allies of big government, trying to block the limited reforms that are the only way to stave off the more sweeping measures favored by the Left.

As genuine conservatives stand athwart history and yell "stop," we need to offer an alternative. The REAL ID Act is the only alternative to a national ID card.

| "The REAL ID Act will do little to en-
| sure America's security."

The REAL ID Act Will
Not Help Control
Illegal Immigration

Cory W. Smith

In the following viewpoint Cory W. Smith criticizes the REAL ID Act, which, among other provisions, tightens the requirements for granting asylum to refugees fleeing political persecution. He contends that the system for granting asylum is already rigorous; the REAL ID Act will simply make it more difficult for those genuinely in need of protection to get the help they need. Smith is legislative counsel for Human Rights First, which was formerly known as the Lawyers Committee for Human Rights.

As you read, consider the following questions:

1. How does America's asylum program work, as described by Smith?
2. How can the government improve its immigration and asylum processes, according to the author?
3. In the author's opinion, how does the REAL ID Act hurt asylum seekers?

This year [2005] marks the 25th anniversary of the 1980 Refugee Act. This important legislation brought our domestic law into conformity with international obligations: to protect refugees in dire need of a safe haven. After the Holocaust, nations painfully acknowledged that too many had closed their borders to refugees fleeing certain death. The United States committed to ensuring that this would not happen again—that America would keep its doors open to those fleeing religious persecution and ethnic cleansing. But that time-honored commitment is now in serious jeopardy as several leading House Republicans advance—under the guise of national security—a misguided piece of legislation known as the REAL ID Act. [The REAL ID Act was signed into law on May 11, 2005.]

Last year, these congressmen took advantage of the intelligence reform bill and tacked on several extraneous anti-asylum provisions that had nothing to do with the important recommendations from the 9/11 Commission's report. Fortunately, these provisions—which would have caused serious harm to refugees—were eliminated from the final law due to the strong opposition by a broad coalition of human rights groups, religious and faith-based organizations, civil liberties groups and a bipartisan group of Congressional leaders.

In late January, House Judiciary Committee Chairman James Sensenbrenner, R-Wis., introduced with great fanfare some of these provisions as part of his REAL ID Act. Rep. Sensenbrenner characterizes the anti-asylum language in his bill as border security that will tighten the asylum system that has been allegedly abused by terrorists. These assertions are incorrect.

The Asylum System Is Secure

The horrific tragedy of 9/11 forced Americans to think of security first. We must make sure that we do not take security risks even as we uphold our national tradition of serving as a safe haven to people fleeing persecution abroad. The United States government, after a comprehensive examination of an individual's case, grants asylum to refugees who prove that

Opposition to the Real I.D. Act

Hundreds of immigration rights and civil-liberties groups have criticized the [Real I.D. Act].... They argue that the national I.D. card will allow cops and corporations to spy on citizens and worry that new databases of personal information will aid identity thieves. Opponents also point out that the new bill could create even longer lines at your local DMV, where clerks will scrutinize everybody who applies for and renews a license.... According to security experts, the new I.D. cards won't make the country any safer and will likely make terrorists harder to catch.

Farhad Manjoo, "Identity Crisis," Salon, May 13, 2005.

they have suffered persecution in the past or have a well-founded fear of future persecution—but not before conducting multiple and rigorous security checks on *each and every applicant.* U.S. law "categorically disqualifies" for asylum persons who have committed certain crimes in the United States or any of a wide range of serious non-political crimes abroad. And it bars persons who are deemed security risks—or suspected terrorists. The asylum system is not rife with security gaps and does not act as a sieve for terrorists to remain in this country.

That's right, *each and every* applicant undergoes extensive security checks—including several with biometric indicators—conducted by the Department of Homeland Security, the CIA, the FBI and the Department of State.

Furthermore, beginning in the early 1990s, the asylum process was overhauled to enhance security by reducing incentives for frivolous filings and for those trying to stay in this country by taking advantage of a backlog. The administrative reform eliminated automatic work authorization for asylum applicants, required the timely processing of applications and mandated personal interviews by trained officers. Then, in 1996, Congress enacted expedited removal, which required that aliens arriving at U.S. ports of entry without proper documentation be mandatory detained and demonstrate a credible fear of persecution before bringing an asylum claim before an immigration judge. The Department of Homeland Security, the agency charged with assessing asylum claims and enforcing our immigration laws, is currently authorized to detain the asylum seeker throughout the application process—a practice that is increasingly frequent since 9/11.

Terrorists Avoid Scrutiny

Rep. Sensenbrenner and other proponents of the anti-asylum provisions have frequently cited examples like Ramzi Yousef from the first World Trade Center bombing, and Hesham Mohamed Hedayet, the Egyptian nationalist who opened fire on the El Al airlines counter at Los Angeles airport. They assert that these documented terrorism cases justify the legislation. But of the small handful of cases cited, the vast majority of the individuals applied prior to asylum reform and *none* received asylum.

Indeed, with the exhaustive scrutiny that asylum seekers are subjected to, one wonders: Why would terrorists purposefully subject themselves to all this scrutiny? Terrorists and others who intend to do harm to this country will choose the path of least resistance—which most certainly is not coming in contact with the rigorous array of security and background checks, biometric indicators, absolute bars to asylum, mandatory detention and expedited removal built into a process that last year [2004] granted asylum to only 29 percent of those who applied.

If Rep. Sensenbrenner sincerely wants to keep America safe, the best way to do that is not to change the burdens of proof—or change standards and definitions that will harm legitimate refugees seeking asylum in this country and send them back to their persecutors to face torture or death. Rather, members of Congress should improve interior enforcement, strengthen security measures and address immigration fraud.

The REAL ID Act will do little to ensure America's security. Instead, it will hurt the most vulnerable—those fleeing repressive regimes—while doing little to make our nation safer. The irony is that many of these refugees are America's friends, fighting abroad for democratic reform, risking their lives to further religious liberty and combating political extremism. Recently, when speaking about immigration and our borders, President Bush admonished the American public to remember that "family values do not stop at the Rio Grande River." Family values do not stop there, nor do they stop in Boston, Atlanta, Miami, Seattle, Los Angeles, or, most importantly, in Washington, D.C. When these individuals and their families face torture or death, when their claims are credible, when they have cleared exhaustive security checks, America should be opening her doors—not closing them.

Periodical Bibliography

The following articles have been selected to supplement the diverse views presented in this chapter.

Steve Brown and Chris Coon	"Illegal Alien Sanctuary," July 1, 2003. www.frontpagemag.com.
Chris Coon	"Open Borders Bus Tour," October 13, 2003. www.frontpagemag.com.
Nick Gillespie	"Barely Illegal," *Reason*, November 13, 2005.
Farhad Manjoo	"Identity Crisis," May 13, 2005. www.salon.com.
Juan Mann	"Bush Now Positively Glorifying Illegal Aliens," January 18, 2005. www.vdare.com.
Matthew Mehan	"El Norte," *National Review Online*, January 14, 2004. www.nationalreview.com.
Joseph Menn	"Federal ID Act May Be Flawed," *Los Angeles Times*, May 31, 2005.
Sara B. Miller	"When Doing the Right Thing Leads to Arrest," *Christian Science Monitor*, January 7, 2004.
John O'Sullivan	"Amnesty Trapdoor," *National Review Online*, January 6, 2004. www.nationalreview.com.
Bill Sammon	"Bush Revives Bid to Legalize Illegal Aliens," *Washington Times*, November 10, 2004.
James Sensenbrenner	"Plan Would Protect U.S." *USA Today*, May 9, 2005.
Jacob Sullum	"ID Card Trick," *Reason*, May 13, 2005.
Wendy Young	"America's New ID Program: Missing the Terrorists, Punishing the Victims," *Global Beat Syndicate*, May 23, 2005.

For Further Discussion

Chapter 1

1. What examples of the harms of illegal immigration does Frosty Woolridge provide? How does Tim Wise refute these points? After reading both viewpoints, do you believe illegal immigration harms or helps the United States?

2. After reading the S.J. Miller and Brian Grow et al. viewpoints, do you believe that illegal immigration is helping or hurting the American economy? Cite examples from either viewpoint to support your opinion.

3. According to viewpoints by Phyllis Schlafly and the Border Action Network, serious environmental and property damage has been done along the Southwest border. Schlafly contends that the illegal aliens crossing the border are at fault; the Border Action Network blames in part the increasing militarization and increased border patrol activity for the problem. Which argument do you believe? Explain your answer.

Chapter 2

1. Daniel Griswold and Peter K. Nunez have different perspectives on who is responsible for illegal immigrant fatalities. Review their viewpoints and give your opinion on the issue.

2. Do you believe the anti-immigration movement is rooted in racism directed at foreigners, as asserted by Emile Schepers? Or is it a result of concerns about America's safety and way of life, as maintained by Tom Tancredo? Support your answers with references to the viewpoints.

3. In her viewpoint, Rachel Meeropol offers examples of illegal aliens being victimized by government policies. Do you agree with her that illegal aliens are being scapegoated by the government? Or is their treatment justified as a part of the war on terror, as asserted by Michelle Malkin? Explain.

Chapter 3

1. Sam Francis writes that the U.S. military should be deployed to the border to prevent the influx of illegal aliens; Gene Healy asserts that such a deployment would be illegal and dangerous. In your opinion, should the military be used in this manner? Explain your answer.

2. According to Tamar Jacoby, a guest worker program with Mexico is a viable compromise in the illegal immigration debate. Do you agree? Why or why not?

3. After reading both Tamar Jacoby's and Mark Krikorian's viewpoints on the guest worker issue, how do you think such a program would impact on the American economy? Explain your answer.

4. Review the viewpoints by Cinnamon Stillwell and Bob Moser about the Minuteman Project. Was the project a good idea? Do you think it seriously impacted the flow of illegal immigration across the border? Explain your answers.

Chapter 4

1. Do sanctuary policies help law enforcement, as asserted by Sheila Jackson Lee? Or do they hinder law enforcement, as claimed by Heather Mac Donald? Explain your answer.

2. Cory W. Smith maintains that REAL ID "will hurt the most vulnerable—those fleeing repressive regimes—

while doing little to make our nation safer." After reading Smith's and Mark Krikorian's viewpoints on REAL ID, do you agree with Smith, or do you think REAL ID is an improvement in America's national security system?

Organizations to Contact

American Civil Liberties Union (ACLU)
125 Broad St., 18th Fl., New York, NY 10004
(212) 944-9800 • fax: (212) 869-9065
Web site: www.aclu.org

The ACLU works to protect the rights and principles delineated in the Declaration of Independence and the U.S. Constitution. The ACLU Immigrants' Rights Project works with refugees and immigrants facing deportation and with immigrants in the workplace. It has published reports, position papers, and the book *The Rights of Aliens and Refugees*, that outline the rights immigrants and refugees have under the U.S. Constitution.

American Friends Service Committee (AFSC)
1501 Cherry St., Philadelphia, PA 19102
(215) 241-7000 • fax: (215) 241-7275
e-mail: afscinfo@afsc.org
Web site: www.afsc.org

Founded in 1917, the AFSC is a Quaker organization that attempts to relieve human suffering and find new approaches to world peace and social justice through nonviolence. It lobbies against what it believes to be unfair immigration laws, especially sanctions criminalizing the employment of illegal immigrants. It has published *Sealing Our Borders: The Human Toll*, a report documenting human rights violations committed by law enforcement agents against immigrants.

American Immigration Control Foundation (AICF)
PO Box 525, Monterey, VA 24465
(540) 468-2022 • fax: (540) 468-2024
e-mail: aicfndn@cfw.com
Web site: www.aicfoundation.com

AICF is a nonprofit research and educational organization that believes massive immigration, especially illegal immigration, is harming America. It calls for an end to illegal immigration and for stricter control on legal immigration. The foundation publishes the monthly newsletter *Border Watch* and several pamphlets, including *Common Sense on Mass Immigration* and *Erasing America: The Politics of a Borderless Nation.*

American Immigration Lawyers Association (AILA)
918 F St. NW, Washington, DC 20004
(202) 216-2400 • fax: (202) 371-9449
e-mail: ilrs@aila.org
Web site: www.aila.org

AILA is a professional association of lawyers who work in the field of immigration and nationality law. It publishes *Immigration Law Today*, a bimonthly periodical that compiles and distributes a continuously updated bibliography of government and private documents on immigration laws and regulations.

Border Action Network
PO Box 384, Tucson, AZ 85702
(520) 623-4944 • fax: (520) 792-2097
e-mail: BAN@borderaction.org
Web site: www.borderaction.org

The Border Action Network is a grassroots membership organization based in Arizona to protect the human and civil rights of people who live in Arizona border communities as well as the Sonora desert along the Arizona-Mexico border. The Border Action Network opposes the anti-immigrant groups that patrol the border in southern Arizona. In 2002 it published *Hate or Heroism: Vigilantes on the Arizona-Mexico Border.*

Brookings Institution
1775 Massachusetts Ave. NW
　Washington, DC 20036-2188

(202) 797-6000 • fax: (202) 797-6004
e-mail: brookinfo@brook.edu
Web site: www.brook.edu

Founded in 1927, the Brookings Institution is an independent, nonpartisan research and educational organization that publishes material on economics, government, and foreign policy. It publishes analyses of immigration issues in its quarterly journal *Brookings Review* and in various books and reports.

California Coalition for Immigration Reform (CCIR)
PO Box 2744-117, Huntington Beach, CA 92649
(714) 665-2500 • fax: (714) 846-9682
e-mail: barb@ccir.net
Web site: www.ccir.net

CCIR is a grassroots, volunteer anti-immigration organization that seeks to ensure the enforcement of the nation's immigration laws. CCIR publishes recent immigration stories, alerts, bulletins, and the monthly newsletter *911*.

Cato Institute
1000 Massachusetts Ave. NW
   Washington, DC 20001-5403
(202) 842-0200 • fax: (202) 842-3490
Web site: www.cato.org

The Cato Institute is a libertarian public policy research foundation dedicated to stimulating policy debate. It believes immigration is good for the U.S. economy and favors easing immigration restrictions. The institute has published various articles on the subject of immigration reform.

Center for American Unity
PO Box 910, Warrenton, VA 20188
Web site: www.cfau.org

The Center for American Unity is a national nonprofit educational organization that conducts research and monitors developments on a broad range of economic, domestic, defense, and foreign policy issues, such as mass immigration, multiculturalism, multilingualism, and affirmative action. It also publishes *VDARE.com*, an online journal that features numerous articles and commentary on immigration reform.

Center for Immigration Studies (CIS)
1522 K St. NW, Suite 820
  Washington, DC 20005-1202
(202) 466-8185 • fax: (202) 466-8076
e-mail: center@cis.org
Web site: www.cis.org

CIS is an independent research organization that studies the effects of immigration on the economic, social, demographic, and environmental conditions in the United States. The center adheres to the view that illegal immigration has become a burden on America and favors reforming immigration laws to make them consistent with U.S. interests. It publishes numerous reports, position papers, and commentary on the subjects of immigration and immigration reform.

El Rescate
1313 W. Eighth St., Suite 200
  Los Angeles, CA 90017
(213) 387-3284 • fax: (213) 387-9189
Web site: www.elrescate.org

El Rescate offers free legal and social services to Central American refugees. It is involved in federal litigation to uphold the constitutional rights of refugees and illegal immigrants. It compiles and distributes articles and information and publishes the newsletter *El Rescate*.

Federation for American Immigration Reform (FAIR)
1666 Connecticut Ave. NW, Suite 4000
  Washington, DC 20009
(202) 328-7004 • fax: (202) 387-3447
e-mail: info@fairus.org
Web site: www.fairus.org

FAIR works to stop illegal immigration and to limit legal immigration. It promotes the view that immigrants into the United States cause higher unemployment and burden social services. FAIR has published many reports and position papers, including *Breaking the Piggy Bank: How Illegal Immigration Is Sending Schools into the Red* and *The Costs of Illegal Immigration to Texans.*

Heritage Foundation
214 Massachusetts Ave. NE
Washington, DC 20002-4999
(202) 546-4400 • fax: (202) 546-8328
e-mail: info@heritage.org
Web site: www.heritage.org

The Heritage Foundation is a conservative think tank that has published numerous articles on immigration in its Backgrounder series and in its quarterly journal *Policy Review.*

Manhattan Institute (MI)
52 Vanderbilt Ave., New York, NY 10017
(212) 599-7000 • fax: (212) 599-3494
e-mail: mi@manhattan-institute.org
Web site: www.manhattan-institute.org

MI is a public policy research organization focusing on taxes, welfare, immigration reform, education, race relations, and urban life. It publishes *City Journal* as well as a number of articles and position papers on the topic of immigration.

National Council of La Raza (NCLR)
1126 Sixteenth St. NW
Washington, DC 20036
(202) 785-1670
Web site: www.nclr.org

NCLR is a national membership organization that seeks to improve opportunities for Hispanic Americans. It conducts research on many issues, including immigration, and opposes restrictive immigration laws. In addition, it publishes and distributes reports and papers on immigration, such as *Immigration Reform: Comprehensive Solutions for Complex Problems* and *Immigration Advocacy and Media Toolkit: A Handbook for Legislative Advocacy and Media Communications.*

National Immigration Forum
50 F St. NW, Suite 300, Washington, DC 20001
(202) 347-0040 • fax: (202) 544-1905
Web site: www.immigrationforum.org

The National Immigration Forum is considered the nation's premier immigrant rights organization. It supports effective measures aimed at curbing illegal immigration and promotes programs and policies that help refugees and immigrants assimilate into American society. It publishes two references on the subject of immigration: *Immigration Basics 2005* and *Basic Immigration Facts,*

National Immigration Law Center (NILC)
3435 Wilshire Blvd., Suite 2850, Los Angeles, CA 90010
(213) 639-3900 • fax: (213) 639-3911
e-mail: info@nilc.org
Web site: www.nilc.org

NILC is a national support center that works to protect the rights of low-income immigrants and their families. It disseminates information about immigration, welfare, and employment law and is a notable resource for immigration attorneys. It conducts policy research, and its publications include the *Guide to Immigrant Eligibility for Federal Programs.*

National Network for Immigrant and Refugee Rights (NNIRR)
310 Eighth St., Suite 303, Oakland, CA 94607
(510) 465-1984 • fax: (510) 465-1885
e-mail: nnirr@nnirr.org
Web site: www.nnirr.org

NNIRR is a national organization that encompasses community, church, labor, and legal groups devoted to the cause of equal rights for all immigrants. These groups fight to end discrimination and unfair treatment of illegal immigrants and refugees. The network aims to strengthen and coordinate educational efforts among immigration advocates nationwide.

Negative Population Growth (NPG)
2861 Duke St., Suite 36, Alexandria, VA 22314
(703) 370-9510 • fax: (703) 370-9514
e-mail: npg@npg.org
Web site: www.npg.org

NPG promotes the view that the United States is overpopulated and that world population must be reduced. It calls for an end to illegal immigration and an annual cap on legal immigration. NPG frequently publishes position papers on population and immigration in its *NPG Forum*.

United States Conference of Catholic Bishops (USCCB)
Migration and Refugee Services, Washington, DC 20017
(202) 541-3208 • fax: (202) 541-3399
e-mail: mrs@usccb.org
Web site: www.usccb.org/mrs

USCCB is comprised of Catholic bishops in the United States and the Virgin Islands. Its program Justice for Immigrants aims to educate the public about the positive aspects of immigration and to advocate for fair immigration laws and policies. On a local level, it has organized networks that assist immigrants with legal issues.

U.S. Citizenship and Immigration Service (USCIS)
Department of Homeland Security
  Washington, DC 20528
(202) 282-8000
Web site: uscis.gov

The USCIS was created in 2003 when the Immigration and Naturalization Service became part of the Department of Homeland Security. It is responsible for administrating immigration and naturalization functions and establishing immigration services policies and priorities. The USCIS Web site is a comprehensive resource for the latest immigration and naturalization news, forms, and announcements.

Bibliography of Books

Cynthia S. Becker *Immigration and Illegal Aliens 2005: Burden or Blessing?* Farmington Hills, MI: Thomson Gale, 2005.

George J. Borjas *Heaven's Door: Immigration Policy and the American Economy.* Princeton, NJ: Princeton University Press, 1999.

Ko-lin Chin *Smuggled Chinese: Clandestine Immigration to the United States.* Philadelphia: Temple University Press, 1999.

Jon E. Dougherty *Illegals: The Imminent Threat Posed by Our Unsecured U.S.-Mexico Border.* Nashville, TN: WND, 2004.

Mark Dow *American Gulag: Inside U.S. Immigration Prisons.* Berkeley: University of California Press, 2004.

Nancy Foner *In a New Land: A Comparative View of Immigration.* New York: New York University Press, 2005.

Gordon H. Hanson *Why Does Immigration Divide America? Public Finance and Political Opposition to Open Borders.* Washington, DC: Institute for International Economics, 2005.

Helene Hayes *U.S. Immigration Policy and the Undocumented: Ambivalent Laws, Furtive Lies.* Westport, CT: Praeger, 2001.

Bill Ong Hing *Defining America Through Immigration Policy.* Philadelphia: Temple University Press, 2004.

Bonnie Honig   *Democracy and the Foreigner.* Princeton, NJ: Princeton University Press, 2001.

Tamar Jacoby, ed.   *Reinventing the Melting Pot: The New Immigrants and What It Means to Be American.* New York: Basic Books, 2004.

Khalid Koser and John Salt   *The Geography of Trafficking and Human Smuggling.* London: Routledge, 2002.

David Kyle and Rey Koslowski, eds.   *Global Human Smuggling: Comparative Perspectives.* Baltimore: Johns Hopkins University Press, 2001.

Michelle Malkin   *Invasion: How America Still Welcomes Terrorists, Criminals, and Other Foreign Menaces to Our Shores.* Washington, DC: Regnery, 2002.

Robert Lee Maril   *Patrolling Chaos: The U.S. Border Patrol in Deep South Texas.* Lubbock: Texas Tech University Press, 2004.

Rob Maury   *Your Rights as a U.S. Citizen.* Philadelphia: Macon Crest, 2003.

Rachel Meeropol, ed.   *America's Disappeared: Detainees, Secret Imprisonment, and the "War on Terror."* New York: Seven Stories, 2005.

Tram Nguyen   *We Are All Suspects Now: Untold Stories from Immigrant America After 9/11.* Boston: Beacon Press, 2005.

Kent A. Ono and John M. Sloop — *Shifting Borders: Rhetoric, Immigration, and California's Proposition 187.* Philadelphia: Temple University Press, 2002.

James L. Outman, Roger Matuz, and Rebecca Valentine — *U.S. Immigration and Migration.* Detroit: UXL, 2004.

Jorge Ramos — *The Other Face of America: Chronicles of the Immigrants Shaping Our Future.* New York: Rayo, 2002.

Daniel Sheehy — *Fighting Immigration Anarchy: American Patriots Battle to Save the Nation.* Bloomington, IN: AuthorHouse, 2005.

Robert Courtney Smith — *Mexican New York: Transnational Lives of New Immigrants* . Berkeley: University of California Press, 2005.

Tom Tancredo — *Open Borders, Open Wounds: What America Needs to Know About Illegal Immigration.* San Francisco: Encounter, 2005.

Frosty Woolridge — *Immigration's Unarmed Invasion: Deadly Consequences* . Bloomington, IN: AuthorHouse, 2004.

Chiso To Yoshido and Alan Woodland — *The Economics of Illegal Immigration.* Basingstoke, England: Palgrave Macmillan, 2005.

Aristide R. Zolberg and Peter M. Benda — *Global Migrants, Global Refugees: Problems and Solutions* . New York: Berghahn, 2001.

Index